DECADES

Focus
in the 1970s
The Music of Jan Akkerman and Thijs van Leer

Stephen Lambe

sonicbondpublishing.com

Sonicbond Publishing Limited
www.sonicbondpublishing.co.uk
Email: info@sonicbondpublishing.co.uk

First Published in the United Kingdom 2021
First Published in the United States 2021

British Library Cataloguing in Publication Data:
A Catalogue record for this book is available from the British Library

Copyright Stephen Lambe 2021

ISBN 978-1-78952-079-8

Typeset in ITC Garamond & ITC Avant Garde
Printed and bound in England

Graphic design and typesetting: Full Moon Media

Acknowledgements

Thanks to Huw Lloyd-Jones, Steve Pilkington,
Gillian Lambe and Libido Chafe

I have derived many of the details regarding album credits,
plus some other factual information, from the sleeve notes
to the *Focus 50 Years Anthology* Box set, released in 2020
by Red Bullet and compiled by the Focus and Jan Akkerman
archivist, Wouter Bessels. I have attempted to credit him
where such information has been extensively used.
Wouter has also given assistance with the editing and fact
correction of this book, so I thank him for his friendly
and professional assistance.

Peet Johnson's fabulous book *Hocus Pocus Focus*
(2015, Tweed Press, 978-0-646-59727-0) was also a major
help in compiling much of the factual information in this
book. It deserves a much wider readership.

Jan and Thijs on *The Old Grey Whistle Test* in May 1972. (*BBC / Red Bullet / Wouter Bessels*)

DECADES | Focus in the 1970s

Contents

Introduction

Music is created in many ways. When a group of musicians join together to become a 'band', the dynamic within that group initiates the music they produce. Sometimes this creativity comes from harmony, sometimes from conflict. Most often, it is a combination of the two. It's different for every band, of course.

Take Jan Akkerman and Thijs van Leer of Focus, for instance. It was the lure of becoming a jobbing musician that, like his English contemporary Rick Wakeman, tempted Thijs away from his formal studies. For Jan, it was the beat boom of the early 60s – albeit the version in his home country – that lured him into professional music. The two musicians were never really friends and were at loggerheads from very early in their musical collaboration. We'll speculate on that shortly. Nonetheless, the tensions between them produced some of the most distinctive and beautiful music of the 1970s. For Jan, it was his bold and experimental take on rock guitar that gave him such a distinctive edge. For Thijs, it was the classics and more specifically, his beloved Bach, which rarely left his influences. It was jazz that led them to meet in the middle, with Jan, in particular, an almost evangelical improviser. This approach also embraced by Thijs – but only up to a point, and it was this which led to some of the tensions between the two. Indeed, when Focus were at the height of their powers, one of the conflicts between the two musicians was about the level of improvisation, with Jan bemoaning Thijs' tendency to play – and indeed yodel – the same things night after night. Jan, however, rarely played in the same way twice. You never quite knew what he was going to do next, which might be both thrilling and terrifying in a live setting.

The fact that their music was almost entirely instrumental gave Focus a universal appeal. While it was considered unwise to attempt to become 'rock stars' without singing actual songs, there has always been a valuable niche for instrumental acts. Think Mike Oldfield or Jean Michel Jarre, for instance, or even the Pink Floyd of the early 1970s, for whom vocals were often a secondary consideration. In an era of vocal groups, Focus really stood out.

It was a star that burned brightly but all too briefly. The band's 'classic' line up – Jan, Thijs, talented rock bassist Bert Ruiter and Buddy Rich-inspired drummer Pierre van der Linden – only recorded one album (*Focus 3*) while the band's masterpiece remains its predecessor *Focus II* (aka *Moving Waves*) on which Jan allegedly played most of the bass parts.

The van Leer / Akkerman partnership lasted for five studio albums in total, while the 1970s incarnation of Focus itself recorded only six (plus a live album and a compilation). Yet even during the band's twenty-five-year slumber, before the Thijs-led revival of the group in the early 2000s, they were never forgotten. Part of this is due to the sheer ubiquity of their untypical, unique piece 'Hocus Pocus' – used in countless TV shows and movies over the years. But this is also due to two other pieces that have also seeped into the public consciousness worldwide – the 1973 European hit 'Sylvia' and their early chart success in the Netherlands, 'House Of The King'. Nobody ever sounded quite like Focus, and it's unlikely anyone ever will do so again.

When I first started appreciating progressive music in the late 1970s, the first incarnation of Focus has already run its course. But for me, two bands stood out from the rest of the pack. They were Yes and Focus. With Focus, it was the sidelong composition 'Eruption' that really captured my imagination. Although there were no lyrics, in my febrile teenage imagination, I *lived* the story of Orpheus and Euridice; my imagination stoked in the same way that 'Close To The Edge' by Yes did. And so I went on my own journey of discovery, buying each album in turn. Sometimes I was disappointed, sometimes I was baffled. However, I was never bored.

This book is a guide to the Focus of the 1970s and the eight albums that were released under this name during that decade. I have borrowed from the Sonicbond Publishing sister-series *On Track* by looking at each track individually. I also take this approach with the Jan Akkerman and Thijs van Leer solo albums – seven apiece – from this period, plus a few records with other musicians, on which the two of them made significant contributions.

Neither musician has quite thrown off the shackles of their famous band. Even in the 1970s, pieces that were originally recorded by the band found their way onto their solo albums, and while Thijs has fully embraced the music of Focus again in the last twenty years, a solo set by Jan is rarely without a version of 'Sylvia' or 'Tommy' to this day. Nonetheless, both musicians produced some interesting and varied solo material up to 1979, which is well worth exploring. That's not to say that their careers beyond the scope of this book aren't also worth investigating, of course. But that's for another time.

Cover Art

Many band's careers are synonymous with their cover art. Focus are not one of those bands. They never had a consistent cover style or logo in the

1970s, and there are very few album designs that have any sort of genuine artistic merit. But they are, at least, distinctive.

Focus Plays Focus / In And Out Of Focus had many different versions, even in the early 70s, all of which feature a picture of the initial line up based around an – at best – mediocre design. *Focus II / Moving Waves* also has two covers. The original one is the psychedelic version, featuring the band and the more familiar sun-dappled lake (or sea) with the musicians inset. I have a lot of affection for this cover, though it's hard to argue that it's a masterpiece. *Focus 3* is also distinctive, if uninspired – a brown, blurred close up of Thijs, with the title in black and white. It has not worn well. Had the band produced the planned album in 1973, one suspects that rather more cash might have been thrown at the design for that platter. As it was, it's somewhat ironic that *At The Rainbow* should have such an expensive production, albeit in Europe only, where a gatefold sleeve with a cut-out portion – which must have cost a fortune – was produced for initial pressings. Inside the gatefold was a bold reproduction of the mural inside the Rainbow venue, which pictures a Moorish village. Later pressings had a much plainer version of the black sleeve, with a tiny picture of the band in the bottom left corner. The US version featured four pictures of the band members on a grey background – it's far less interesting.

Given that the 1970s saw the height of expensive, conceptual cover design, one might have expected an artist to have a bit of fun with a title like *Hamburger Concerto*, but in the end, elegance was the order of the day, so we have a gatefold sleeve with a textured cover design in black and white, and the album title in mock-neon. Inside the gatefold were pictures of the band in an elegant 18th Century location. *Ship Of Memories* (a blurred image of a battleship with an arriving – or perhaps attacking – plane) and *Mother Focus* – a bizarre collage – are both just odd, while *Focus Con Proby* returns to the cod-elegance of *Hamburger Concerto* but with rather less success. Would a more cohesive and imaginative set of album designs have influenced Focus' commercial success? Probably not, but the lack of consistency does irritate.

It's understandable that Thijs and Jan's solo albums should focus rather more on the musicians themselves. The concept behind Thijs' *Introspection* series was simple. Take a photo of the artist with or without a flute – and there's your cover. The only difference between them is Thijs hair length – and hairline. *O My Love* has a high-concept gatefold, very pink and very 1970s. Some might consider it hideous. I couldn't possibly comment. The proggiest cover on any of the albums discussed in this book is, ironically, *Nice To Have Met You,* which has a surreal cover painted by Richard Hess. Two well-dressed men meet in a woodland, but their heads are hands, which are in the middle of a handshake. It's an odd cover for a jazz-funk album!

As for Jan, both *Profile* and *Tabernakel* feature simple, full-face portraits, as does *Aranjuez,* while *Eli* features an elegant photograph of the two protagonists. The most bizarre cover is the eponymous debut album, featuring Akkerman in bed with an acoustic guitar, which is scratching his back via a very feminine arm. While it has been seen by many as iconic, to me it's odd and slightly creepy, although Wim Ballendax's logo is very powerful in a 1970s way. *Live* sees a black-clad Jan playing a hollow-bodied Gibson – very much the jazzer – while *3* has a white-clad Jan superimposed on a stretch of water, his shadow a guitar – so now he's the funkateer.

Jan Akkerman and Thijs van Leer

Jan Akkerman and Thijs van Leer were – and remain – very different people. However, despite their obvious difference in personality and upbringing, there are obvious parallels between the two musicians. For instance, both came from Jewish backgrounds, although whether this factor directly affected their careers in any sort of major way or not is unclear. Both men were strongly supported in their early careers by their parents, who were also musicians. Thijs came from a well-off family who encouraged him in his efforts to become a classical musician. Jan was supported throughout his early career buy parents who did their best to make his early bands successful. Both musicians received a broad musical education, with jazz at the centre. Thijs discovered modern jazz in the early 1960s, while Jan was raised on the music of Django Reinhardt, as well as absorbing many more varied ethnic styles within his more cosmopolitan and working-class upbringing.

The reasons for the personality clash that blighted their relationship may well stem from this difference in class and background. There's plenty of evidence to suggest that the two were are loggerheads from time to time, even in 1970. However, the differences also stem from their attitude towards their music. As we've already discussed, Jan – something of an intense character – is an evangelical improviser. When recording his solos for 'Eruption' Mike Vernon notes that Jan never played a solo the same way twice. As a result, playing the same material over and over for years on end – as Jan was requited to do particularly during the band's 'hard-touring' years from 1972 to 1974 – immensely frustrating; even dispiriting. Jan's true musical 'soulmate' may well have been Yes' first guitarist Peter Banks, perhaps a less talented player than Jan, but equally committed to the 'purity' of spontaneity. Many of Peter's later recordings and his improvisational trio Harmony In Diversity – which the author saw live in the mid-2000s – demonstrate this.

Jan found Thijs' lack of commitment to improvisation immensely frustrating. Yet, there's no doubt that, listening to many of the band's live tracks, Thijs – as a jazzer himself – was no stranger to improvisation. It's just that he was more comfortable with improvising in the planned sections of pieces like 'Anonymus II' and 'Eruption'. As a showman at heart, Thijs' was much more comfortable and satisfied with playing the same pieces night after night.

With this in mind, it is almost astonishing that their collaboration lasted as long as it did – from 1969 until the start of 1976. From 1973 onwards, they rarely played in the same room when recording and stood a long way apart on stage. Additionally, Jan was not interested in the trappings of becoming a public figure, whereas Thijs was much more comfortable with such things. Perhaps it was displacement activities – his growing interest in music for the lute and – in 1975 particularly – his minor obsession with playing through a talkbox guitar effect and well as a growing interest in the rhythm box, that kept Jan engaged.

Understanding the tension between improvised and written music is essential to understanding what made Focus – and specifically the musical relationship between Jan and Thijs – tick. Improvisation works best in a modestly-sized live setting, in which a symbiotic relationship between artist and audience can flourish. Jazz, for instance, works best in small clubs, where the audience can enjoy the relationship and spontaneity between the players. As rock music shifted through the gears in the 1970s and later in the 1980s, moving into bigger and bigger venues, this was gradually lost and audiences needed bigger shows and bigger sounds to make the experience worthwhile, since you could no longer see the interaction between the players in any sort of detail.

On recorded media, extensive improvisation also needs tempering since the audience only has one sense to experience what is happening – its sense of hearing. This is why, as I will explain later in this book, I feel that 'Eruption' is a masterwork, but that 'Anonymus II' is overcooked. The former is beautifully structured to fill one side of vinyl perfectly. It has a beginning, a middle and a satisfying end. That the band often wandered from that structure in live performance, I find frustrating. 'Anonymus II', however, feels like a well-structured studio jam. It would have been great to have experienced it in the studio at the time, but do we really want to listen to Bert's bass solo again and again? Your money may vary, of course. This is just the author's perspective, and for many, the fact that Focus jammed with great skill is a source of immense pleasure. Music appreciation is completely subjective, after all.

Jan Akkerman

Jan Akkerman was born in 1946 into a working-class family. His parents – Jacob and Gerda – were both musicians, and Jan's first instrument was the Accordion. His first guitar was a triplex Egmond, which he purchased with a friend. Further practice took place with a neighbour, Tata Mirando, who played with The Royal Gypsy Orchestra, and who taught him about

Django Reinhardt, a very early influence.

Jan formed a rhythm and blues band called The Friendship Sextet at the age of eleven with a certain Pierre van der Linden, playing covers of 1950s hits. He had the full backing of his proud parents, who helped clothe and manage the band. After a period in Salzburg and Vienna, a teenage Jan formed a new band called Johnny And His Cellar Rockers, named after Jan (Johnny) and the Akkerman residence's cellar in which they rehearsed. This new group was influenced by The Shadows but also Indo-rock, a fusion of Eastern and Western styles created by immigrants living in Holland. Jan's parents continued to support the band, as did his uncle Jaap, while his brother Cocky played rhythm to Jan's lead guitar. After a year, Pierre joined the band (to leave a year later) and in 1961, the instrumental group were offered a contract by Decca. The band went on to considerable success in the Netherlands playing instrumental music in the early and mid-1960s, later morphing into Johnny and the Hunters, and even later, The Hunters. Successful singles were recorded with vocalists Rita Severijnse and Floortje Klomp.

After The Hunters folded in 1968, Jan recorded his first solo album *Talent For Sale* that same year but opted to work for his father's scrap metal business as well as playing the odd session. However, another opportunity was to come along in 1969, with the formation of the short-lived (as far as Jan was concerned at least) progressive blues combo Brainbox, which reunited him with Pierre, as well as featuring future collaborator Kaz Lux. The band's eponymous first album was a big hit in the Netherlands. The world, surely, was his for the taking …

Thijs van Leer

Thijs van Leer was born in 1948 in Amsterdam to an affluent middle-class family. Both his parents were musicians with classical training. Steeped in serious music from an early age due to his father Ed, from the age of six Thijs studied piano with Maria Stroo of the Dutch Royal Concertgebouw Orchestra, having been introduced to the instrument by his mother Mary at the tender age of three. Thijs first composition was 'Uncle Willy', a tribute to a family friend who had helped his father – who was from a Jewish background – escape Nazi-occupied Holland and study the flute in Switzerland.

Thijs continued his piano studies throughout childhood but found it hard to concentrate on many of the set pieces. He already had the compositional bug. He also played harpsichord in the school orchestra, conducted by his father. At the age of thirteen, he began flute studies under his father, whose principal advice was to concentrate on making a beautiful noise rather than to focus on technique.

In 1962, Thijs discovered jazz, loving much of the modern canon, although he was especially fond of Miles Davis. The talented and versatile youngster joined his first jazz group, The Raoul Angenot Quintet, while continuing his classical studies, including lessons in musical arrangement with Rogier van Otterloo, to become so important to Thijs a little later in his career. At eighteen, Thijs the polymath won inter-school prizes in drama improvisation, jazz, and classical. He also won a prize in the 'Dutch song' category, performing the self-penned 'Nooit Zal Ik Vergeten (De Nachten Samen Met Jou) (Never Shall I Forget The Nights Together With You)'. Amazingly, this song was even released as a single.

Not confident enough in his musical abilities to continue his studies, Thijs went to the University of Amsterdam to study Art History, where he continued to develop his interest in the dramatic arts. It was during rehearsals for a production of John Webster's *The Duchess Of Malfi* that Thijs learned that Ramses Shaffy, a well know musical entertainer, was looking for backing singers for his upcoming cabaret show. Could this be a way into the entertainment business for Thijs?

The Stars Align

It is 1968. For Jan, the Hunters have just dissolved, while Thijs is looking for opportunities in the music industry.

Thijs was initially unsuccessful in his attempts to get into Ramses Shaffy's troupe, but perseverance paid off. At the time, Thijs was living at home with his parents in Hilversum, and when advised by Shaffy that if he could get to the singer's base in Amsterdam in 40 minutes, he'd get an audition, Thijs borrowed his mother's car and made it in time. He passed the audition and joined the other backing singers Sylvia Albers (later to be immortalised as the muse for a massive hit single), Marjol Flore and Eelko Nobel. He also occasionally played flute. This was a hugely influential period for Thijs. The show and the resulting album – called *Shaffy Chantant* – was a strange, groovy combination of French chanson, jazz and various ethnic folk musics. It was hugely theatrical and informed the extravagant stage presence that Thijs was to employ throughout his subsequent career.

During this period, Thijs also recorded his second single, 'Zolang De Wereld Nog Draait (As Long As The World Still Turns)', a Dutch language cover of the Engelbert Humperdinck hit 'Les Bicyclettes de Belsize' which, in turn, in September 1968, led to an invitation to join a group of musicians who would play a weekly spot on Catholic Radio Broadcasting (KRO). This group also included drummer Hans Cleuver and bassist Martijn Dresden. Although hired as a flautist, Hans encouraged Thijs to add organ to the group's appearances, and the trio soon began jamming together.

The three musicians became Trio Thijs van Leer, which, in turn, was asked to provide the backing to Ramses Shaffy's next project, *Shaffy Verkeerd*. Opening in January 1969, this was an extravagant, contemporary cabaret, which featured songs like 'MacArthur Park' and Bob Dylan's 'I Shall Be Released'. Once again, Thijs was learning about stagecraft. In the meantime, the Trio also supplemented their income recording TV and radio commercials, and in the Summer of 1969, left the cabaret to concentrate on their own gigs. Initially, they played covers and were particularly influenced by the music of current proto-progressive rock band Traffic.

When Martijn suggested that they hire a guitarist to broaden their sound, Thijs was not initially interested. Indeed, an eighteen-year-old Eef Albers had been jamming with the band on the houseboat on which Thijs now lived. When Thijs heard Jan and spoke to him about his own compositions and the ethos behind the band, he started playing with them.

Meanwhile, Jan had been playing with Brainbox and the band's debut had been released to some acclaim. This is a pivotal album in the development of 'classic Focus' and there are certainly plenty of hints towards the path that the band that would come follow within a couple of years. Particularly noticeable is the swinging, jazzy relationship between Jan and Pierre, and while the recording itself is a little rough and ready, the lineage is obvious. The side-long improvisation on 'Sea Of Delight' presages the sort of approach that Jan would use on 'Fresh Air', 'Eruption' and 'Anonymus II', for better or worse.

There are, understandably, various accounts as to how Jan came to leave Brainbox, but the most likely explanation seems to be that the band's manager, John Boete van Setten, was keen to bring in a more extravagant guitarist in terms of stagecraft. He had seen Peter Banks of Yes play, a man with an expansive and mobile stage persona, even if it did occasionally affect the accuracy of his playing. Jan, on the other hand, was always – in Brainbox as well as later in Focus – a less mobile performer, letting his fingers do the talking. It seems likely that the manager was looking for a reason to get rid of Jan and that his jam sessions with Trio Thijs van Leer were the excuse the manager had been looking for. Jan suggests that he was dissatisfied with the progress that Brainbox was making musically and was looking to leave. There's probably truth in that account, too.

'Elektrisch Levenslicht' (single) – Neerlands Hoop In Bange Dagen
Personnel:
Thijs van Leer: keyboards,
Jan Akkerman: guitar
Hans Cleuver: drums
Martijn Dresden: bass
Freek de Jonge: vocals
Bram Vermeulen: vocals and piano
Produced by Frans Boelen
Recorded by Andre Hooning and Pierre Geoffroy Chateau at Intertone Studios, Heemstede, August 29 1969. (Thanks to Wouter Bessels for credits)
Available as part of the *Focus 50 Years Anthology*

However, the first time the band performed on record as a four-piece was was on 29 August 1969 as the backing band to this 'crazy' Dutch musical comedy team, one of a number of acts becoming notorious for a multimedia approach to their art during this hugely creative period. As a song, this piece is not much to write home about. The band were booked as individuals rather than as a 'band' as such. However, as a calling card for the band that would become Focus, it is rather excellent. The band are tight and well recorded, with all four players given little moments in the spotlight. There's a repeated motif in the arrangement that has the band stop on a dime to allow Jan and Thijs (on organ) to play a unison riff that has more than a hint of classic Focus about it. The piano on the song's outro (although probably played by co-vocalist Bram Vermeulen) also makes giving the track a spin worthwhile. Available on YouTube for some time, the song makes a welcome appearance on the *Ship Of Memories* disc of the *Focus 50 Years Anthology*, released in 2020.

Enter Ramses
The band also backed Ramses Shaffy, and the four musicians were next asked to play on his forthcoming album *Sunset Sunkiss*. Rehearsals took place at Kasteel Groeneveld in Baarn near Hilversum from July to September 1969 to become the band's permanent rehearsal space, a beautiful – if spartan – location, freezing in winter. Although not yet billed as Focus, the resulting album combined Shaffy's experimental monologues with the beginnings of the Focus 'sound'. The first side has music credited to Sextet Thijs van Leer and featured the Trio with Jan playing as a session musician, not part of the sextet. It's worth checking out on Youtube, but in truth, it's not an easy listen. There are elements of jazz and rock, of course, but the overall effect is somewhat attritional, particularly for an English speaking audience, who will be able to make little sense of Shaffy's Dutch language monologues. Side two featured the Trio only but is an expansive, psychedelic affair including a lengthy flute solo from Thijs and traces of music that would be reused in Thijs' composing with Focus. The band played the composition live later in the year, with Jan also commencing work on his next solo album, to become *Profile*.

However, it was Martijn again who provided the contacts to further the tentative four piece's career, and via his father, he made contact with Hubert Terheggen of Radio Tele Music (RTM) who signed the group to his production company, arranging for an album to be recorded in London the following year. In November 1969, the band first played as Focus at the Bird's club in Rembrandtplein. The set mainly included covers, including *Concierto de Aranjuez*, but the group's eponymous title track also made its first appearance in a live setting. However, with cash always short, the band accepted an offer to become the pit band for notorious new musical …

1970 – Focus Play Focus

If we were to stumble across the members of Focus in very early January 1970, what might be their circumstances? For a start, it's most likely they would be freezing. The four members of the band were acting as the pit band for the Dutch production of *Hair* in a tent near the Olympic Stadium on the outskirts of Amsterdam. This was not ideal for any of them, least of all, one must imagine, Jan, for whom playing the same mundane arrangements night after night must have been something of a trial. But it was paid gig, and it did allow them to rehearse their own live set during the day – and all day on Monday, which was a day off for the show.

Those that have heard the Dutch soundtrack to the 1970 production of *Hair* (the author could not track it down) suggest that there's almost nothing of the Focus that we would come to know and love in this recordings. The show did allow a free-for-all improvisation with the audience allowed onstage at the end of the show, however, allowing the band to let off steam. It was around this time that the group name of Focus was first coined. As Thijs told Peet Johnson:

My mother was reading a philosophy book to me when I was young, and she said, in English, 'to focus upon' and I asked her, 'what is 'to focus upon'? She said it means 'to direct, to concentrate'.

It's a beautiful name. It creates an image of a nice, warm, cosy family, but I also wanted to focus on the human mind. I thought that there is perhaps a form of music that can be a catalyst to help people focus and deal with their own problems [as opposed to music that acts just as a way of blotting them out].

These were high ideals indeed and not lacking in pretension. But there is little doubt that no band has ever sounded quite like Focus, even if – ultimately – such ideals were only occasionally fulfilled in practice. The book his mother quoted from was written by Hazrat Inayat Khan, the Indian-born musician, teacher and founder of the Sufi order, who we will meet again as the lyricist of 'Moving Waves' via one of his poems.

'The Shrine Of God' (Shaffy) b/w 'Watch The Ugly People'
(van Leer, Shaffy) – Ramses Shaffy With The Focus Band
Personnel:
Ramses Shaffy: vocals

Thijs van Leer: keyboards, flute
Jan Akkerman: guitar
Hans Cleuver: drums
Martijn Dresden: bass
Produced by Hans van Hemert
Recorded by Albert Kos at Phonogram Studio, Hilversum, 6 and 16 October, 25
November, 4 and 16 December 1969, 7 January 1970. (Thanks to Wouter Bessels
for credits)
Available as part of the *Focus 50 Years Anthology*

The first official usage of the name Focus was on a single release by Thijs'
old boss, Ramses Shaffy. Recorded at the end of 1969 and completed in
very early 1970, 'The Shrine Of God' b/w 'Watch The Ugly People' was
released later in 1970, before the band's debut. It was credited to 'Ramses
Shaffy Met Band Focus', so it warrants a proper entry here.

Despite having their band name on the cover of the single, there's very
little on 'Shrine Of God' to mark out Focus as the startlingly original outfit
they were to become. Shaffy's vocals, too, are decent but do not suggest
that he was anything except a fairly standard baritone crooner of the type
so often found at the time. Indeed, he's often on the verge of losing pitch
during the song. It's Jan's work – prominent if untypical – that stands out,
his jangly guitar very much 'of the time', with some very fine lead work
buried on the mix towards the end of the song, including a few licks that
sound very similar to his work on the first Focus album, for which the
band were rehearsing at the time. The song itself is hardly distinctive – a
somewhat repetitive plea for religion to be found in the hearts of men
rather than in formal places of worship.

Both Thijs and Martijn are more prominent on the B-side 'Watch The
Ugly People', with Thijs far more involved. This is hardly surprising since
Thijs wrote the music for this rather better – if short – song. He features
on organ and Mellotron, giving the track a spacey feel, while Martijn's
bassline is also crucial, and Jan plays rhythm guitar throughout. The lyric
implores the listener to avoid those that are ugly – ugly on the 'inside',
of course. No self-respecting lyricist would have a pop at physically ugly
people in the late 1960s!

Focus Play Focus / In And Out Of Focus (1970)
Personnel:
Jan Akkerman: electric and acoustic guitars

Thijs van Leer: piano, Hammond organ, Mellotron, flute, lead vocals (except 'Happy Nightmare'
Martijn Dresden: bass, trumpet, lead vocals on 'Happy Nightmare', backing vocals
Hans Cleuver: drums, percussion, backing vocals
Wouter Moller: cello on 'Happy Nightmare'
Produced by Hubert Terheggen
Recorded by Jerry Boys at Sound Techniques Studio, London in January 1970
Highest chart placings: Netherlands: did not chart, UK; did not chart, USA: 104
Available as part of the *Focus 50 Years Anthology* or on Red Bullet CD

The band's debut album was recorded at Sound Techniques Studio in Old Church Street, London, in January 1970. The dates had been set up by Hubert Terheggen, who acted as de facto producer on the album, although it is clear that his role was much more of an executive producer's one and that – in effect – the band self-produced the album with the help of engineer Jerry Boys. This was probably not a good idea, and the album production feels mushy – very much a product of the 1960s rather than the 1970s.

Not unlike the debut Genesis album From Genesis To Revelation, this formative recording, which was somewhat unsuccessful, has had many re-issues over the years. Your author's vinyl copy is the 1973 Sire US edition, which misses out the vocal track 'Sugar Island' completely. This seems to have been due to its rather disparaging view of the 'Sugar Island' in question – Cuba – at a time when US relations with Castro's Communist regime were beginning to thaw. As a result, I had never heard the track at all before researching this book!

It is very clear that at this stage of their early development, Focus were not quite sure what sort of band they wanted to be. Of the seven tracks released initially, five have traditional 'song' structures of sorts, although the vocals – shared between the band except for Jan – are most definitely a weak link. Although Thijs was later revealed to be a better 'vocaliser' than a singer, per se, there are no vocals even to rival the confidence of his performance on 'Moving Waves' (the song). Instead, the 'strength in numbers' principle is adhered to, with vocals shared or double-tracked throughout. However, on the two instrumental pieces, there are some powerful suggestions of what was to come just a year or so later. The rhythm section is impressive, and Martijn Dresden, in particular, can consider himself very unlucky not to have been in the revamped band formed at the end of the year – a victim of circumstance rather than lack of ability. However, both Jan and Thijs show what fledgeling talents they were, with terrific performances. One aspect of the album that is impressive – but didn't really carry across into later performances – is how well Thijs uses organ and piano in combination, particularly in the longer instrumental pieces.

Eight tracks were recorded during those January sessions in London. One, 'Spoke The Lord Creator' was not released until the 1975 out-takes compilation *Ship Of Memories*. The 1971 Dutch reissue replaced 'Focus (vocal)' with 'House Of The King', of which more in a moment. The CD issue begins with 'Focus (vocal)', whereas the vinyl versions open with the instrumental version. Wouter Bessels finally produced the definitive running order in the *Focus 50 Anthology Box* with 'House Of The King' as a bonus track, whereas other CD versions include it in the main running order – although that track wasn't released on vinyl in the UK until *Focus 3* in 1972. Confused? We'll use the current CD version of the album as our guide, with 'House Of The King' as an 'official' bonus and 'Spoke The Lord Creator' added for convenience. If you have the CD, you can play the album in any order you like!

'Focus (Instrumental)' (van Leer)

This track set the template for the regular Focus pieces that graced most of the band's albums up to the present day. It takes the melody of the main song, which we will look at shortly and improves it considerably by giving it to Jan's lead guitar – which make the first couple of minutes a restful delight – over Thijs organ and piano. The first transition arrives thereafter but just teases us before a repeat of the main melody. It's stirring stuff, very much in keeping with the band that we know and love. The piece develops pace eventually into something of a jam, with Jan soloing powerfully and with considerable skill around a specific guitar figure, even if his guitar sound is a touch reverb-heavy. The piece slows slightly while Thijs solos on flute around the same figure, while Jan throws in some choppy rhythm guitar, as the flute takes the piece to its conclusion.

The second half of the piece, skilfully played though it is, is less interesting than the first. The first transition is thrown in and then discarded, whereas I could have taken a few more uses of that. It's quite possible that the band of 1972 might have made more of the various potential different sections of this piece, rather than simply soloing. Nonetheless, it's an impressive opening (or closing) of the album.

An excellent version of the track, recorded by live sound engineer Cocky Akkerman (Jan's brother) at Sarasani, Den Burg (Texel), is available on CD2 of the *Focus 50 Years Anthology* box set.

'Why Dream' (van Leer, Eric Cleuver)
Thijs and Martijn share lead vocals on this slice of late 1960s whimsy, with lyrics by Hans' father Eric Cleuver. There are strong whiffs of both Pink Floyd and The Kinks in the vocal melody and the arrangement, which has Jan quite effective on acoustic and lead guitar, and his lengthy solo at the end of the song is excellent, even if the song itself is somewhat slight. The pronunciation of the English lyrics is also poor – understandable in the circumstances, but hardly increasing its appeal to an international audience.

'Happy Nightmare (Mescaline)' (van Leer, Dresden, Mike Hayes)
Ah, a bossa nova! This is hardly progressive, but the song is rather pleasant, with the only real 'lead vocal' – by Martijn Dresden – on the album. He does a decent enough job, too, his vocal charmingly vulnerable, even if the backing vocals from Thijs and Hans are less impressive. It does have a great intro, with Martijn singing over Jan's sensitive acoustic guitar and cello. Then the bossa nova rhythm begins, and the song takes on a different character. The keyboard arrangement is interesting, with organ, piano and Mellotron all used sensitively, while Jan's jazzy guitar accompaniment reveals how versatile he could be. His choppy jazz solo, towards the end of the song, is delicious, and Hans' drumming is also his most impressive on the album. We end on acoustic guitar and cello again. It sounds nothing life Focus, but it is … nice!

'Anonymus' (van Leer, Akkerman, Dresden, Cleuver)
Side two begins with 'Anonymus' (sic), which is built first around a piece from the 15th Century Burgundy Court in France, which has (surprise, surprise) no known author. It's called 'Dit Le Bourguignon' and it bookends this piece. We begin with trumpet (via Martijn) and drum, before we launch into the piece proper, which is a ripe and powerful blues jam built around its riff (presumably written by Jan). Again, this is

the direction that the band would choose to go in, and Thijs flute solo that begins the piece is particularly impressive, as is his blues piano solo (with hints of the classics) which follows. Martin delivers a decent bass solo before Jan cuts in with searing rock guitar and there's even time for a – mercifully brief – drum solo with a final flurry of guitar to finish as the piece slows in a walk, demonstrating what a classy live outfit the band already were. This piece was clearly recorded live in the studio, with some later overdubs.

One final note: The piece finishes with a reprise of 'Dit Le Bourguignon', this time played on overdubbed flutes with echoed handclaps. However, due to a tracking error on both the *Best Of Focus* and *In And Out Of Focus* CD versions, this brief coda is actually placed at the start of 'House Of The King', meaning that it is impossible to listen to 'House' as a standalone track without a bit of 'Anonymus' shoved at the start of it. This is very, very irritating. Thankfully, the *Focus 50 Years Anthology* corrects this error, and this has now also translated over to the remastered version of the compilation itself. Phew.

'Black Beauty' (van Leer, Eric Cleuver)
A splendid instrumental introduction descends into a rather mundane and poorly executed vocal piece, once again rooted in the late 1960s. The arrangement is good, with Jan's guitar excellent, as is Thijs' piano. The vocals just don't work, though Martijn's trumpet solo is a nice touch, as is the key change right at the end of the instrumental section. But this is poor stuff in the main

The lyrics are quite 'right on' even for the era. They are about a love between a white man and a black woman, using Solomon and Sheba as a metaphor. It's all somewhat heavy-handed, but given that this was their first album, we'll let them off!

'Sugar Island' (van Leer, Dresden, Jan Staal)
Who on earth is this? This song couldn't sound less like Focus, though it does have a rather lively South American flavour. It's sung almost competently by Thijs and might have made a passable single had it not been for the anti-Castro lyrics. There's a good, if brief, solo from Jan and another on flute by Thijs, while the jazzy, 'babadaba' refrain may charm some and irritate others. It's all quite catchy while being at the same time a bit nondescript. A better singer at the time – even Shaffy – might have made more of it.

'Focus (vocal)' (van Leer, Eric Cleuver)
The album ends (or begins, depending on your version) with the vocal version of 'Focus'. In this version, Jan's lyrical guitar is replaced by a unison vocal performance that seems to lack confidence and converts a rather beautiful opening into something of a dirge. The vocal section lasts less than a minute, before a gentle drift to the end with some single-note volume control antics from Jan. As a stand-alone track, it's something of a waste of time, but as an album closer, as the bookend with the instrumental version as the opener, it does have some logic to it. Overall, it's not great, though.

Additional tracks:
'House Of The King' (Akkerman)
See below.

'Spoke The Lord Creator' (van Leer, Eric Cleuver) – released on *Ship Of Memories*
This track was recorded on 26 January 1970 as part of the first album sessions, so features the original line up including Martin Dresden and Hans Cleaver. After a promising Bach-inspired start (hinting at 'Starter' from 'Hamburger Concerto'), the piece descends into some somewhat uninspired country rock. It's not quite clear whether it's a dull instrumental or a cluttered backing track. Whichever it is, it's brief and uninspired, though does have some nice guitar work from Jan. There are also hints of 'One For The Road' from *Hamburger Concerto*, although the author will admit to not having spotted it until it was pointed out to him!

Hair Today, Gone Tomorrow
Having had the – understandably – thrilling trip to London to record the album, the band had another project to record in the Netherlands. However, this was the less enticing prospect of the soundtrack to the Dutch production of *Hair*. This, they could have recorded in their sleep. Thijs and Jan also appeared on an album by Robin Lent, one of the *Hair* troupe. Thijs and the rhythm section also recorded part of an album with folk singer Bojoura, the nom de plume of Raina van Melzen, who was later to marry Hans.

However, their time in the *Hair* tent was drawing to a close, as the band were getting more and more opportunities to perform as Focus, with Hans or Gerda Akkerman on the constant lookout for gigs. The

band finally moved on in June 1970, when the production went on tour –
planning eighteen months playing around the Netherlands – and another
combo took over. Focus were now free to play their own gigs whenever
they wanted. A Focus set from around this time might have featured a
variety of instrumental material on top of some pieces from the debut
album. The band mixed jazz, rock and the classics, featuring a few Miles
Davis pieces, a jazzy take on the English folk tune 'Scarborough Fair' –
popular at the time through the hit rendition by Simon and Garfunkel
– and the centrepiece of the set, a version of *Concierto De Aranjuez* by
Rodrigo.

The debut album remained unreleased for several months. Nonetheless,
they did make it to the final of a competition called 'Barbarela de
Conjunctos 70' on the island of Majorca in Spain. Progressing to the
final on 11 June, Focus were only given fifteen minutes to play, meaning
that they would need to lose a small section of their chosen piece, the
aforementioned *Concierto De Aranjuez*. Learning that a local stitch-
up by gangsters meant that Spanish group Los Bravos were already to
be winners even before the event took place, Focus played the whole
seventeen-minute piece in the hope of a second-place finish. However,
at the fifteen-minute mark, the organisers pulled the plug. Outraged,
Jan, Hans and Martijn trashed the dressing room while Thijs distracted
the audience by waltzing through the tables, playing his flute. The local
constabulary was called, and the band spent the night in jail, making
some newspaper headlines in the press to boot.

Thijs suggests that Jan wrote their best piece of work to date the day
after their night in prison, whereas Jan suggests his muse may have been
a Spanish airline stewardess during the band's stay in Spain. Whatever
the inspiration, it was to mark their breakthrough – in the Netherlands at
least.

The original trio – without Jan – also played at the Concertgebouw in
Amsterdam in June 1970, where they also backed Ramses Shaffy. The
band took part in an experimental multimedia event involving orchestra
and ballet as well as a live rock band. The performance also featured live
projections of artwork by famed Dutch artist MC Escher, later to make
his mark in the progressive rock world as the designer of the cover to
Emerson, Lake and Palmer's *Brain Salad Surgery* album. Part of the
programme for the performance was *Symphony Number Five (aka
Time Spirit)* by Dutch composer Jurriaan Andriessen, with a 65 piece
orchestra conducted by Rogier van Otterloo. Such performances were

not uncommon in 1970, as progressive blues morphed gradually into progressive rock. Bands like The Nice, Yes and Deep Purple pioneered the combination of classical orchestra and rock music with varying degrees of success before progressive rock acts realised they did not need full orchestras to create symphonic soundscapes as the 1970s wore on.

'House Of The King' (Akkerman)

Personnel:
Jan Akkerman: electric and acoustic Guitars
Thijs van Leer: keyboards, flute
Martijn Dresden: bass
Hans Cleuver: drums, percussion
Produced by Tim Griek
Recorded by Andre Hooning at Intertone Studios, Heemstede, July 1970
Highest chart places: Netherlands: 10, Belgium: 27
Available as part of the *Focus 50 Years Anthology* or CD versions of the debut as well as mosts compilations

The band needed something to give themselves a boost and perhaps a catchy single might do the trick. As a result, the track was put together during the Summer of 1970 at the EMI-Bovema Heemstede studio in Heemstede in one all-night session. It was recorded by Brainbox producer Tim Griek without the permission of Terheggen, who was furious that the band had gone behind his back, but soon relented when he heard the finished piece.

It's short but hugely famous. A hit only in the Netherlands, it has since gone on to worldwide recognition, second (probably) only to 'Hocus Pocus' in terms of recognition by the wider public, even if many people think it's by Jethro Tull! It's catchy melody and upbeat, positive arrangement, meant that it was used all over Europe as a TV theme, most notably on two shows in the UK fronted by TV scientist Magnus Pyke *Don't Ask Me* and *Don't Just Sit There,* between 1974 and 1980. It was also used – rather more ironically – as one of the themes to *Saxondale*, a vehicle for British comedian Steve Coogan, in the mid-2000s. In the show, Coogan plays a vermin exterminator who had once been a roadie for rock bands in the 1970s.

The first thing to say is that it's much better recorded than the album. Jan's acoustic guitar is dynamic and effective, and Thijs main melody line – played on flute – is wonderfully catchy. At less than two and a half minutes, it's all over very quickly but is also beautifully crafted. Note the handclaps, for instance, adding to the percussive rhythm, and also the way Jan's lead guitar doubles the flue melody the second time through. It's simple fare, so the main part of the track lasts only 90 seconds. However, a slower, bluesy guitar solo acts as a bridge before the final reiteration of the main flute theme, and we're done. It's sheer genius.

Although Akkerman has the composer credit, there are suggestions that Thijs may have written the main flute melody – which has always been vociferously denied by Jan. The truth is probably that Thijs made some contributions to a team effort, with Jan the main composer. The track was originally to be another vocal piece, with lyrics by Mike Hayes. However, only the title from his intended version remains. 'House Of The King' is in the first line of his words. Thank goodness wider heads prevailed, though. This is one of the pieces that made the band.

The *Focus 50 Years Anthology* provides two early mixes of the track. Both versions present, essentially, the backing track with keyboards, acoustic and rhythm guitars, bass and drums. Neither feature the flute melody or Jan's solo, and so are interesting in that they illustrate how the piece was built up (including hand claps). Neither are likely to receive multiple plays by any listener but are useful signposts to the final mix.

All Change

By the end of the Summer, 'House Of The King' was in the can, but, like the album, not yet released. The record company smelled a hit. But all was not well within the band. The problems seemed to be two-fold. First of all, Martijn was struggling with a double-whammy of growing drug dependency and parents who disapproved of his choice of profession. It was clear that, sadly, a change was needed. Jaap van Eik, later to be a member of Trace, was auditioned and offered the position. Seeing at first hand how poor relations already seemed to be between Thijs and Jan, he declined.

The other problem was Jan. The ever-restless guitarist was already beginning to get itchy feet. In particular, he was missing playing with his Brainbox bandmate Pierre van der Linden. When a certain bassist and vocalist, Cyriel Havermans, put down some vocals on Jan's ongoing *Profile* project, an understandably twitchy Terheggen had his contributions removed, smelling a rat. Two possibilities became apparent. Either Jan would form a new band away from – and possibly instead of – Focus, or that Pierre would join Focus as the new drummer. Stories do differ at this point, and it's quite possible that several things were going on at once. It does seem that Jan left the band for a while to form a new one with Pierre and that the ever-pragmatic Focus management had to find a solution to keep their investment intact. This turned out to be reuniting the two most distinctive members of the band – Jan and Thijs – while leaving out Martijn (who wouldn't have lasted long anyway) and Hans, who was simply unlucky not to be Pierre. For Thijs, this was a bad time. He, Martijn and Hans had been playing together since 1968, far longer than they had with Jan. Thijs had won his musical spurs with his two friends. It seems that he had little choice – he could either join Jan or see the whole project go up in flames. The involvement of Thijs was not Jan's idea, it has to be said. He was happy to split with Thijs completely, as the personality issues which was to blight their relationship over the next five years had already become apparent. However, Jan eventually said yes to management's plan and as far as he was concerned, Thijs would now play in 'his' group. In one move, Focus was saved, and the power balance in the group was altered for the next few years.

At the same time, Terheggen stepped back from the day to day management of the band and asked Yde de Jong to become the group's manager. The two rejected members of the band responded in very different ways. Martijn reacted very poorly, and given his already fragile state of health and mind, he never recovered. He suffered bouts of addiction and mental illness before becoming a hobo. Hans, while distraught and bitter, kept his life together and was to become Thijs personal manager due to his undoubted business acumen and 'people' skills. He also set up a hugely successful drum school.

Ironically, seeing the potential of 'House Of The King', and with de Jong working hard for the band as their first full-time manager, the Dutch Imperial label signed the band, releasing the album in September 1970. However, it was Seymour Stein at Sire Records in the USA that recognised the true potential of the group worldwide, releasing the album as *In And Out Of Focus* with 'House Of The King' added. And that famous track itself? It reached number ten in the Dutch charts when released as a single right at the end of 1970. At last!

1971 – The Bridge

Focus II / Moving Waves (1971)

Personnel:

Jan Akkerman: electric and acoustic guitars, bass

Thijs van Leer: piano, harmonium, Hammond organ, Mellotron, soprano flute, alto flute, vocals

Cyril Havermans: bass, vocals

Pierre van der Linden: drums

Produced by Mike Vernon

Recorded by Jerry Boys at Sound Techniques Studios and Morgan Studios, London

Recording dates: 13 April to 14 May 1971

Highest chart positions: Netherlands: 4, UK: 2, USA: 8

Available as part of the *Focus 50 Years Anthology* or on Red Bullet CD

> Melody, energy, delicacy … It's timeless.
> **Jerry Boys (recording engineer)**

This new 'version' of Focus found itself with an altered power dynamic, with Jan Akkerman – having initiated this line up in the first place – now taking on equal status with Thijs. The most important realisation for this new four-piece was that they were effectively an instrumental band. Initially, Cyriel Havermans had been recruited as he considered himself a singer-songwriter, and for a brief time, it was thought that he might become the band's vocalist, but the band's emphasis soon changed in the direction of instrumental material, a situation which probably contributed to his early departure from the group.

Havermans did not contribute directly to the sound of *Focus II / Moving Waves*. Indeed a debate had raged over the years as to how much of the album he actually plays on, with Jan contributing either 'almost all' of the bass or, as other sources would have it, just a bit here and there. There's no doubt about the quality of the bass playing on the album; it's superb, moving in the direction of the virtuosity that Bert Ruiter was to bring to the band within the year, so my guess is that it's largely Jan. However, one musician who did make a huge contribution to the band's 'new' sound was drummer Pierre van der Linden. Focus have had a variety of drummers over the years, but nobody brought the same level of Buddy Rich-style jazz intensity to the band. His playing was – and remains – unique.

The final piece of the puzzle was the inspired recruitment of Mike Vernon as producer. Vernon was already a veteran of the British blues scene, having won praise for recording Fleetwood Mac and John Mayall's Bluesbreakers. Crucially, he was considered responsible for the unique atmosphere that had helped make 'Albatross' by Fleetwood Mac such a massive instrumental hit. This became something of a blueprint for the early Focus. As well as allowing the band a timeless, natural 'live' sounding recording quality, Vernon was also crucial in giving the band's magnum opus 'Eruption' it's structure, piecing together sections of the band's composition into a 23-minute work with a genuinely beguiling yet powerful structure. Without him, the band would not have become the success it did. Vernon makes these points in the booklet for the *Focus 50 Years Anthology* Box Set:

Everything was pretty much rehearsed, except for the solos. Jan never played the same thing twice; that was not part of his make up. Except for the melodies, for which the scores were put on paper. There's a lot of solos on this album. The ones we did choose were those that we thought were the best choices at the time.

As a producer, I had to be able to catch the essence of the band live and get it into record. That's what I enjoyed doing. The studio was fairly spacious to create that live sound, so that helped.

Having recorded all the pieces, then it was like Christmas. Unwrap all the presents, and in the end of it, you have this incredible picture.

Moving Waves has been the most successful album I've ever been involved in.

The resulting album was eventually a huge hit, but not instantly – reaching number two in the UK charts in early 1973, a full year after its initial release. The album also made the top ten in Holland and – crucially – in the USA in early 1973.

If the reader will indulge a moment of rabid eulogising, this is – for me – one of the greatest albums of all time and one of the outstanding achievements of the progressive rock era. It's *almost* perfect, and as a result, its lack of complete perfection makes it all the more loveable. It's an astonishing advance over the debut, and while the band themselves must take mist of the credit for this, Vernon should also take some of the plaudits. That they did this in 1971, when many of their progressive contemporaries were not to do their best work for another year or so –

should be noted. Was it to be downhill from here? The band's next two albums also feature highly in 'best Focus album' polls. Yet for this author, this was the bands finest moment – and the decade was only one year old.

'Hocus Pocus' (Akkerman, van Leer)
This version was released as a single in edited form in the Netherlands. Highest chart place: 12

This is the piece that most represents Focus in the minds of the wider public. Indeed, it is one of those rare pieces of music that remains better known than the band that created it. For many, it's unusual structure and, indeed, its unusual sound palate – particularly Thijs' now-famous yodelling and high register, wordless vocals – make it something of a novelty track. What is true is that it is completely unrepresentative of the band yet still informed many of the pieces that came after it, with Thijs taking many an opportunity to yodel on subsequent albums. Most bands – had they come up with Jan's killer riff – would have placed it into a much more conventional hard rock song. Yet Focus – never a band to do the conventional thing – built something else around it completely. Despite the personality clash that had already begun to make itself felt between Jan and Thijs, here is an example of the two working in harmony to produce something completely unique. It's bonkers, of course, but after hundreds of listens, I still find it a lot of fun. Speaking of fun, the track is so unique it bears breaking down into its component parts, so here goes:

0.00: Initial riff on guitar only on the left side of the stereo, joined by lead guitar on the right. Drum fills followed by bass at 0.19. Two guitars and bass play riff in unison. The riff ascends followed by solo toms to:
0.52: Descending yodelling and organ refrain, with some bass. Falsetto ascent (copying the ascent played by the guitar earlier)
1.22: Bass trills lead back into main guitar riff as before, but with more expansive drumming continued into a brief and complex drum solo, then:
1.44: Repeat of yodelling section as previously, but no bass trills this time; instead we have:
2.05: Guitar solo played over the main riff, ascending again via drum solo to:
2.37: Bizarre vocal and organ improvisation, ending with four tom beats into:
2.53: The main riff is repeated, plus a drum solo as before, into:

3.22: Yodelling and organ refrain, ascending again to:

3.44: Second, slightly different guitar solo which ascends via drum solo, this time focusing on the kick drum and snare, to:

4.15: A Flute solo, heavy on the reverb, which becomes a duet, playing a variation on the main riff, leading to:

4.28: A brief tom-tom introduction to the main riff yet again, then another drum solo is accompanied by a rising whistling sound, leading us into:

5.02: A brief section of...er...whistling and accordion, again playing a variation on the main riff, leading – via a short and simple burst of toms, to:

5.12: Another, somewhat wilder and less precise guitar solo over the main riff, with added crowd noise for a few seconds. The band intensity has noticeably increased, as if building to a climax (a masterful touch), reflected in a more intense drum solo, leading one last time into:

5.42: Yodelling and organ, as before, via a more complex bass run once again into:

6.04: The main riff, but with Thijs delivering a manic laugh at the back of the mix. The riff continues and, just after a short drum solo played mainly on toms, the track ends on a single, unison note.

Although clearly a genuine collaboration between Jan and Thijs, with Jan's iconic riff at the heart of every note, it should be noted that at no stage are both musicians playing together. The main riff is played on two guitars throughout (unless one of them is soloing), whereas, when played live, the organ was necessary to fill out the sound left by the lack of the second guitar. Many drummers have played this track over the years, but so unique is Pierre's playing style that the performance only feels 'authentic' when he is involved. Mike Vernon's studio trickery is also crucial, particularly his use of reverb to add atmosphere. These are signs of a true master at work.

'Hocus Pocus' is one of those pieces of music that has seeped into the public consciousness worldwide. It's use by Nike, during the 2010 world cup, for instance, produced a short, drum-heavy remix and an EP that gathered together every available version. It's still available on Spotify. Meanwhile, the piece was also used in the 2017 action movie *Baby Driver*, leading to another – somewhat more Hip-hop orientated – remix. It's a funny old world.

An edit of the six-minute album track was used for the Dutch hit single in 1971. Other hit versions – and subsequent uses on TV and film – have tended to use the 1972 re-record, which we will look at shortly.

'Le Clochard' ('Bread') (Akkerman)

My goodness, what a contrast. This beautiful short piece, written and played by Jan on classical guitar with Mellotron strings from Thijs (producing an effective, otherworldly shimmer as the instrument so often does), is quite exquisite. A brief section quotes Rodrigo's *Concierto De Aranjuez,* part of the band's live set in 1970. The chord structure is far from conventional, so while there is no doubt beauty in this piece, it's also a touch other-worldly, never settling into comfort and requiring the listener's attention throughout.

Jan named the piece 'Le Clochard' – French for hobo or tramp – after one such person he met in the South of France. 'Bread' means what he tried to give him – either actual bread or it's slang meaning, as in money.

'Janis' (Akkerman)

Here we have true collaboration with this lush, full-band ballad. Jan gives the main melody to Thijs' flute, which then becomes a small orchestra of overdubbed instruments. Jan's lightly picked electric guitar accompaniment also helps set a languid tone, suggesting warm summers in the countryside. It's all relatively simple fare, with the entire piece played and then repeated, with a brief coda, to fill its three minutes. It works wonderfully, though. Jan named the track for Janis Joplin, with whom he had played with Brainbox in 1969.

'Moving Waves' (van Leer, Inayat Khan)

It's understandable that the band should still be trying out styles, and the title track is very much the odd man out of the album. Here, Thijs sets part of a poem written in 1923 by the founder of the Islamic Sufi movement's founder Hazrat Inayat Khan to music and sings it himself. His piano accompaniment is beautiful – essentially a classical piece reminiscent of French composers like Debussy, and his heavily-accented lead vocal is actually rather pleasant, too. But the song jars stylistically – it doesn't really belong here. At under three minutes, however, on such a groundbreaking album, we'll allow this short diversion.

'Focus II' (van Leer)

If 'Hocus Pocus' will forever be the band's calling card in the eyes of the wider public, then for me, this is the single track that most represents what the band are all about. Written by van Leer, there is again generosity of arrangement here, as the main melody is given to Jan, although Thijs' keyboards – piano, Mellotron and organ – are prominent throughout. Jan's playing is lyrical and extremely emotional during the main theme, but it's the effortless jazzy sections that really impress, and here the star of the show is Pierre, whose astonishing drumming propels the piece with incredible agility. If any instrumental is capable of tugging at the heartstrings, it's this one and after hundreds of listens over the years, 'Focus II' still moves me to this day, particularly its rising crescendo at the end.

'Eruption'

Focus had originally planned to build a long track around Bela Bartok's *Concerto For Orchestra,* but were unable to get the rights from the composer's estate. While live versions of the track still contained such material, the band instead turned to Gluck's opera *Orfeus and Euridice* for a basic structure to the piece, while borrowing some musical ideas from Montiverdi's *L'Orfeo.* Let's not forget that this side-long piece was recorded in the spring of 1971, a year before Yes' 'Close To The Edge' or 'Supper's Ready' by Genesis, making it one of the very first long-form, break-free, side-long works of progressive rock. While Thijs came up with the main musical themes, it was up to Mike Vernon and engineer Jerry Boys to splice everything together.

The results? To me, this is second only to 'Close To The Edge' in the pantheon of side-long tracks of the 1970s, and aside from a few wordless vocals, it's both entirely instrumental and very varied. It takes the tendencies of the band to want to jam – as shown to a greater degree on the following album *Focus 3* – and hones this into a side of music that is both beautifully structured and accessible. It is genuinely one of the crowning glories of the progressive rock era. Jerry Boys talks about the challenges of putting the track together as part of the *Focus 50 Years Anthology*:

There were no computers in those days, so we had to do the final mix in one go with all hands manually on the mixing desk. The other thing was the effects on Jan's guitars. Especially on 'Eruption' there were quite dramatic mood changes within the middle of the piece he was playing, from quite driving to melodic and soft. He could make different sounds by changing the pick-up switch.

One of the joys of the *Focus 50 Years Anthology* box set is that it includes several versions of the complete piece during the time that it was being developed and as it changed after the release of the album. An astonishing 37-minute version, recorded in the summer of 1970 in Amesterdam and featuring the original line up, has many of the parts as they were finally to appear intact, but no 'Tommy' (for instance). Another version, recorded with a newly-arrived Bert Ruiter and Pierre van der Linden in Rotterdam in October 1971, includes a jazz section and extended guitar, flute and drum solos before ending without rounding off the track as it does on the album. It's a bold 45-minute plus piece and worthy in its own right, even if it does largely depart from the recorded piece from ten minutes in. Let's look at the recorded piece in detail:

a. 'Orfeus' (van Leer)
This is a low-key, neoclassical opening, Thijs' organ stately combining with Jan's electric volume swells, leading to:

b. 'Answer' (van Leer)
The 'Answer' theme is played quietly on organ, then on guitar, before the whole band come in with organ and guitar playing in unison. The piece continues with an angular section, suggesting Emerson, Lake and Palmer, with guitar and organ again in unison, while the bass winds around them both. Back into:

c. 'Orfeus' (van Leer)
A reprise of the first version of this piece, with added toms and a cymbal crash. Leading once again, into:

d. 'Answer' (van Leer)
A shorter reprise of the 'Answer' theme, followed by a brief drum solo, which takes us into:

e. 'Pupilla' (van Leer)
Mellotron and choral vocals (from Thijs and Cyril) with a short and delicate melodic jazz solo from Jan act as a languid introduction to:

f. 'Tommy' (Tom Barlage)
Released as a single in a slightly expanded edit.
Highest chart place: Netherlands: 18

As thrilling today as it was when it was first released, this solo from Jan – based on a theme borrowed from Dutch composer Tom Barlage – is astonishing, not for its speed, but for its lyricism and feel. Jan's Gibson is on the verge of feeding back throughout the solo, and the momentary howl a few seconds in may technically be a mistake, but the track is all the better for it. As this section is less than two minutes long, the main solo was edited so that it was repeated when the song was released as a single. Accompaniment is via organ and Mellotron.

Added much later in the writing process, to place this section into the piece at this particular moment is a moment of sheer genius. The live version from 1970, when 'Eruption' was very much in development, shows that while 'Pupilla' worked perfectly well without it, this 'interruption' provides a real hook for the listener early in this long piece.

While Jan would usually play this piece with all its feedback-inducing ferocity, he was also capable of startlingly different interpretations, as shown during the band's May 1972 appearance on the *Old Grey Whistle Test*, when he plays it in a much more restrained, jazzy style, although this may have been down to volume limitations in the tiny studio.

The solo ends and segues into a short reprise of:

g. 'Pupilla' (van Leer)
Followed by:

h. 'Answer' (van Leer)
A very brief, urgent reprise of the angular section of 'Answer':

i. 'The Bridge' (Akkerman)
A new rising and falling theme introduces Jan's piece, the longest on the album. Effectively, it's a jam, albeit a short one, brilliantly edited by Vernon. Jan begins by soloing in a fast blues style over an organ vamp from Thijs. The solo itself is hit and miss stuff, but it's great to hear a musician of his quality improvising in this way. A reprise of the unison theme is followed this time by an organ solo by Thijs. It sounds more 'worked out' than Jan's but is equally effective, and the bass playing on this section (presumably by Jan) is spectacular. The piece changes tack with some unaccompanied soloing from Jan, leading into:

j. 'Euridice' (van Leer, Eelko Nobel)
This is the first appearance of this lovely new theme, originally written by

former Shaffy Chantant band member Eelko Nobel, played on piano with melodic lead guitar from Jan, then taken up by Thijs' flute. As it comes to an end, Thijs' flute seems to call 'Euridice', before:

k. 'Dayglow' (van Leer)
Thijs' and Cyril's voices are multi-tracked as a Gregorian choir, accompanied by organ, as the piece takes a new twist before more volume-swell guitar from Jan. Again, this is wonderfully melodic stuff, the voices enhanced by the Mellotron. This segues into a brief moment of heavy rock (with added feedback) before the instruments fade, leaving only drums:

l. 'Endless Road' (van der Linden)
I am no fan of drum solos on studio recordings, but here Vernon wisely uses the editing knife, so this excellent solo doesn't outstay its welcome, thus threatening to make the piece unlistenable. As an atmospheric interlude, it's actually very effective. I can't think of any other drum solos that do that.

m. 'Answer' (van Leer)
A reprise of all three main themes in sequence begins with a brief moment of 'Answer' before another brief burst of:

n. 'Orfeus' (van Leer)
And then:

o. 'Euridice' (van Leer, Eelko Nobel)
The piece finishes gently on a reprise of this lovely theme, played quickly on guitar then flute, before ending in a volley of fading drums. The storm has passed.

1972 – Questions and Answers

After a Winter rehearsal session – working on new material and the live set at Kasteel Groeneveld – Focus kicked off 1972 with their first foray into live performance in the market that was considered to be the most important one in Europe – the United Kingdom. New manager Yde de Jong correctly surmised that the nation would be receptive to the band's music and approach, and while the musicians were not convinced, a tour of small club venues took place between 15 February and 10 March 1972. Focus tackled the power crisis taking place in the UK at the time by hiring their own generator. While it was to be later in that year that the band would make a rather more sudden and lucrative impression on the country, invaluable groundwork was done during this tour, even if the band hardly made a penny as a largely-unknown quantity.

Shortly after this tour, the band had their first, day-long session at Olympic Studios in Barnes, London. There they recorded a new single 'Sylvia' and it's B-side, the lyrical 'Love Remembered'.

Thereafter, the band returned to Holland to continue playing live and further develop new material, with both a vocal version of 'Spoke The Lord Creator' and 'Focus III' making their live debuts. The band played the Pinkpop Festival in Geleen, Limburg on 22 May, with the band's version of 'Hocus Pocus' recorded by a Dutch TV crew. A week later, the band were a no-show (for purely 'administrative' reasons) at the Lincoln Festival in the UK but were able to make their first appearance on the *Old Grey Whistle Test* TV show in the UK, then with Richard Williams hosting. That the band played live at all is interesting. Most acts performing in the tiny BBC studio in which the show was recorded at the time had to mime, just out of practicality, although by 1972 this was starting to change. There was a little doubt that some momentum was starting to build, with the band voted 'Brightest Hope' in a June *Melody Maker* poll, ahead of David Bowie and The Electric Light Orchestra, no less!

For Yes guitarist Peter Banks, writing in his 2001 memoir *Beyond And Before*, it was quite an experience supporting Focus in the Netherlands during 1972, with his then-band Flash. His account gives an interesting insight into how problematic playing live anywhere could be, particularly in smaller club gigs, during the early 1970s. He also became a firm fan of the band, helping them to gain some media coverage in the UK, and was hugely impressed by Jan in particular:

I remember the gig; we were on before Focus, and we didn't know who they were or anything. Focus were unknown in Britain at the time and totally unknown in America. But they were very big in Holland, and maybe Germany. I recall there was a large gap between when we went off stage and Focus came on. The crowd was very noisy, and everyone was drunk. Also, the equipment kept breaking down, so it was kind of chaotic. I remember actually standing on the side of the stage, ready to leave, when Focus came on. Well, I was absolutely amazed at the quality of the band. Luckily, I had my little Sony mono tape machine and microphone with me. So I taped the whole gig. It still is a very special gig to me. Jan Akkerman's guitar playing was just incredible. I'd never seen anybody play quite like him. He had all the tricks in the book and played like a cross between Django Reinhardt and Julian Bream. Akkerman was just coming out with this stuff. And he played some of the things I'd played, like the triplet stuff and little riffs, and things. He was doing the volume pedal thing without the volume pedal! Jan was doing it with the volume knob on his guitar. That absolutely amazed me — I had never seen this done before. He was such a soulful player.

So that was my first introduction to Jan Akkerman. And again, I do remember the gig being pretty chaotic. The equipment kept breaking down, and the house PA kept going down. Focus came on, and then off, and then on again. And I remember a few bottles were thrown — it was kind of a lively night. I met Akkerman that evening, and later on, Focus came over to England. I called up Chris Welch at *Melody Maker* and told him how wonderful this band Focus was. I said to Chris, 'You have to interview these guys and do a story on them.' I guess I was kind of spreading the word about Focus because I loved the band.

But as it turned out, the first release in 1972 was not from the band itself, but the first solo album from Thijs, which was to become something of a record-breaker.

Introspection – Thijs van Leer (1972)

Personnel:
Rogier van Otterloo: arrangements, conducting
Luc Ludolph: recording engineer
Thijs van Leer: flute
Ruud Jacobs: producer

Letty de Jong: voice
Recorded 1972
Highest chart positions: Netherlands: 1, UK: did not chart, USA: did not chart
Current availability: Music on CD Cd or BGO double edition with *Introspection II*

As if Focus weren't busy enough in 1972, Thijs was also asked by his conservatoire mentor Rogier van Otterloo to record an album of what can best be described as 'light classics,' for the CBS label as a flautist only. Very much pitched at the popular classical market in an era when such divisions were not quite so carefully delineated as they are now, this turned out to be a masterstroke. The final product – which featured compositions by Faure and Bach as well as two by van Otterloo – also cleverly tapped into the Focus back catalogue by including rearrangements of 'Focus I' and 'Focus II'. The resulting product was a massive success, becoming the best selling Dutch album of all time for a while.

None of the albums in the *Introspection* series have dated particularly well, and much of what made them popular seems a little trite today, but there's little doubting the skill involved. Otterloo's orchestral arrangements, dominated by waves of Mantovani-style strings, are lush but also somewhat (as Jan observed) overblown. Also, the vocals of light soprano Letty de Jong, although beautifully sung, are very much in a style popular in the late 60s and early 70s. At best, they add a pleasant texture and at worst, they are cringe-inducing. However, Thijs' lyrical style of flute playing was just about perfect for the project. What you make of this album will largely depend on whether you can see past the textures that have dated badly, and there are a lot of these. In particular, the string arrangements are occasionally over the top in a way that may have suited the 'easy listening' audience of the time.

Suit its audience the album certainly did. The album entered the Dutch charts on 1 July, reaching number one and staying in the charts into 1973. Its selling power reached well beyond Focus' rock audience and made Thijs a household name in his home country. It was *that* successful.

A quick note about Letty de Jong. Readers will note that in all my reviews of the *Introspection* series, I am a little dismissive of her contributions. This is entirely based on the way her voice is used on these albums, which in terms of arrangement, has dated somewhat poorly, and not on the quality of her singing. Indeed, Letty had a long and successful career as a vocalist in the Netherlands, where she was known for the purity of her voice. She was much in demand for radio and TV commercials, and often recorded with her composer husband Cees Smal. She died in 2008, aged 71.

'Pavane (Op. 50)' (Gabriel Fauré)

We kick off in typical style, with Fauré's 'Pavane'. It's a popular – perhaps over popular – tune to kick the album off with, and the lush string introduction grounds us before Thijs' flute carries the main melody. Two minutes in, however, we have acoustic and bass guitar, and some vocals placed sympathetically back in the mix – to begin with at least – although the 'la la la' vocal line is somewhat more intrusive. It's all rather melancholic and lovely, and while the string arrangement is somewhat overblown as expected, here it works and the balance of all the textures is just about fine.

'Rondo' (van Otterloo)

This original 'dance' from van Otterloo starts well enough, Thijs duelling with an unnamed oboe player. But then there are more 'la la la' vocals, Swingle Singers style, causing this listener's buttocks to clench somewhat. Nonetheless, it's rather splendid, except the vocals, and there are – hopefully unwitting – references to the traditional British tune 'The British Grenadiers' in there somewhere. This brief track was – not surprisingly – released as a single, backed with a non-album track called 'Siciliana'.

'Agnus Dei' (From Mass in B minor) (Johann Sebastian Bach)

This piece begins impressively, with a restrained string arrangement and stately harpsichord line. Even when Letty comes in, her vocals are respectful to the track and work reasonably well. One of the reasons these arrangements were so popular is that the emphasis, as always, is on the melody. Thijs doesn't arrive until a couple of minutes in, doubling the melody being played by the orchestra while Letty sings a counter melody. It's a fairly successful and respectful rendition, all in all, building to a rather emotive climax.

'Focus I' (Thijs van Leer)

Side one finishes with the first van Leer composition, a rather pleasing version of the original Focus tune. We begin with piano, acoustic guitar and flute playing the main melody, which works very nicely. The high pitched strings are something of a distraction, as are Letty's 'la, la, la' vocals once again. The transition into the second part of the piece – the jazzier section – is a touch clunky, but once achieved, it could have been persevered with longer before a return to the lush main melody – a fault with the Focus original as much as anything. It's all rather good and actually quite faithful to the original, bar Letty's vocals.

'Erbarme Dich' (from St. Matthew Passion) (Bach)
By the time we return to Bach at the start of side two, the formula is in place, and we know what to expect. Here, Thijs flute carries the main melody with another reasonably well judged counter melody from Letty and a tasteful string and harpsichord arrangement. It's a longer piece and doesn't really go anywhere much, so it does overstay its welcome by a couple of minutes at least.

'Focus II' (van Leer)
If, like me, you revere this piece above pretty much all others in the Focus canon, you may be wary of this version, given what has already taken place here. In truth, having only one featured lead instrument – Thijs' flute – does mean that the piece does lack the emotion of the original, and the over the top, piercing string arrangement may also cause a few missed hearbeats. Not to mention the effect of Letty's jaunty 'la la la's'. Indeed, the piece really misses a drummer as the famed transitions on the original are again rather clunky once again. Thankfully the main melody sees the piece through to a fade-out which includes an actual flute solo.

'Introspection' (van Otterloo)
Credited to van Otterloo, this final piece in fact, more than hints at Albinoni's famous 'Adagio In G Minor' melody, but otherwise is a fitting climax to the album. Almost all the textures already featured are thrown in here, including piano, bass and guitar. There are even some restrained drums – to a rather over-lush orchestral arrangement, while Letty's vocals are more restrained, thank goodness. Thijs largely doubles the main melody played by the orchestra.

Focus 3 (1972)
Personnel:
Jan Akkerman: electric and acoustic guitars, lute
Thijs van Leer: organ, piano, harpsichord, alto flute, piccolo, vocals

Bert Ruiter: bass
Pierre van der Linden: drums
Mike Vernon: backing vocals on 'Round Goes The Gossip', tambourine on 'Sylvia'
Produced by Mike Vernon
Recorded by George Chikantz at Olympic Sound Studios, Barnes, July 1972
(except the single versions of 'Sylvia' and 'Love Remembered' recorded in March 1972)
Highest chart places: Netherlands: 1, UK: 6, US: 35
Available as part of the *Focus 50 Years Anthology* or on Red Bullet CD

With the profile of the band all over Europe on the increase, they returned to the studio in July 1972 to record their third album. Studio B at Olympic in Barnes was once again their studio of choice, which had been chosen in conjunction with Mike Vernon and had already been used when they recorded the as-yet-unreleased single 'Sylvia' back in March. The studio was chosen as the band were after a heavier sound which would allow them to play together 'as live'. Jan even had a sound stage created to enhance the live vibe. The presence of Bert Ruiter to the band cannot be overstated here, as at last, the band has a bass player who could match the other musicians in terms of virtuosity. If the band wanted to record as a live unit, it could now do this with a minimum of overdubs. Indeed, the vast majority of the material was recorded in this live setting. Some guitar and flute (particularly) were overdubbed later. You can clearly hear this on the final product.

The album was recorded in four days – an astonishingly quick turnaround considering that they were able to produce a double album. It's fair to say that the band were well prepared going into the studio, and once set up, they were able to get their material down on tape in very quick time.

So, to the album itself. The decision to make it a double was crucial, and it remains much loved amongst Focus fans. There's little doubt that it contains some of the band's strongest and most representative material. The required 'heaviness' is certainly there – not that this is a metal album – but there's a presence to the production that's not quite there on *Focus II / Moving Waves*. Jan's guitar particularly benefits from this quality. I will be controversial, however, in stating that the album would be even greater had the band stuck to their initial plan to make a single album. How would I change it? By putting 'Elspeth Of Nottingham' onto side one (perhaps as an opener) and by removing 'Anonymus II' completely, leaving 'Focus III' and 'Answers? Questions! Questions? Answers!' to fill the second side. In short, in my view, the monster improvisation that is 'Anonymus II' doesn't bear up to repeated listens and would be better relegated to 'bonus material' status.

There's little doubt that Focus were a hugely confident live band at this point and that their improvisational skills were second to none. Whether those skills should be expressed in such an extensive way on a studio album is the key. What might be thrilling to an audience in a live setting may not be so exciting with multiple plays of a vinyl record or a CD. *Focus 3* has two pieces that contain extensive sections of such improvisation, albeit in highly structured form. For me, 'Answers? Questions! Questions? Answers!' is enough. To take an existing track – 'Anonymus' – from the band's debut, and use that as the basis for a brand new studio track – including lengthy bass and drum solos – covering an astonishing 27 minutes of vinyl – seems excessive, even at a time when such excesses were not uncommon. Even so, I have encountered few tracks recorded, even during this time of exploration and innovation that was the 1970s, that need to be interrupted so that a vinyl record could be turned over.

Despite my reservations over the inclusion of 'Anonymus II', there's little doubting the ability of the band to put together excellent – some might even suggest 'perfect' – 'sides' of music. Side one here – 'Round Goes The Gossip' to 'Carnival Fugue' – is as good a sequence of shorter tracks as they were ever to commit to vinyl, rivalled only (arguably) by the first side of *Hamburger Concerto*.

We will deal with the tracks as they appear on vinyl versions and the release of the *Focus 50 Years Anthology*. The original vinyl version of this double album famously pushed part of 'Anonymus II' onto side four of the vinyl and British versions completed this short side with 'House Of The King', which had not yet appeared on a UK album at that stage, but that track was dealt with earlier in this book.

'Round Goes The Gossip' (van Leer)

I have already suggested that 'Focus II' might be the archetypal Focus piece, but this stupendous opener runs it a close second. The track opens with a brief drum swirl, before the band enters in a quirky and endearingly jazzy refrain, with a heavily echo-drenched van Leer (and Mike Vernon) singing the title over and over again. Immediately, the 'heavier' sound is evident, with Jan's Les Paul full and fruity. This is the band in full, angular prog rocking mode. Only the drum sound disappoints slightly. There's a short pause in which Thijs sings a section of *The Aeneid* by Virgil (from whose work the title comes) – in Latin. This may sound pretentious, but Thijs's typically-quirky falsetto delivery makes it sound anything but, and we pitch straight back into the main piece. At just over three minutes in, there's a frenetic jazz section, with guitar and organ trading lightning-fast licks and Pierre's drumming at its best. The piece – just over five minutes long – ends with a reiteration of the main theme, with ascending shouts of 'round goes…' to a fade-out. This spectacular and breathless piece of music is full of confidence and a fair amount of charm. Nothing else in the progressive rock canon, or indeed in the Focus discography, sounds quite like it.

'Love Remembered' (Akkerman)

Jan's only piece on this first – spectacular – side of the album is this gloriously melodic and gentle piece of music. Yet it's also a true collaboration, as the lead instrument here is Thijs' sensitive and beautiful flute. Despite that, Jan's classical guitar – with suggestions of the Flamenco style – is crucial, as are Pierre's percussion interjections as the piece builds. The little subtle moments of reverbed synthesiser also help suggest a romantic summer day, located wherever you need it to be, but in Jan's case, in Friesland. Despite its gentle nature, it's an intensely happy piece of music and Thijs' jazzy flute run just after two minutes is one of his most exquisite instrumental moments on any record, in my opinion.

'Sylvia' (van Leer)
Released as a single B/W 'Love Remembered.'
Highest chart places: Netherlands: 9, UK: 4. USA: 89

And so we come to one of the three pieces ('Hocus Pocus' and 'House Of The King' being the other two) for which the band will also be best known. It is titled, playfully, after its muse Sylvia Albers, who performed alongside Thijs as part of *Shaffy Chantant* in 1968, when the melody was originally written. It's clearly a piece that was meant to have a vocal line and it does indeed have lyrics, written by Dutch actress Linda van Dyck. In 1968, the song had a real mouthful of a name: 'I Thought I Could Do Everything On My Own, I Was Always Stripping The Town Alone'. To which someone with English as their first language might say 'pardon?'

However, what might have been a trite and ordinary song is here transformed into a true classic of instrumental pop music to rival Vernon's other great production, 'Albatross' by Fleetwood Mac. Indeed, there's something timeless about the arrangement. The introduction builds over a short period, building just a touch of tension, released when Jan's beautifully played lead line arrives, carrying the melody through its various repetitions, alleviated at just the right moment by Thijs' 'la la' falsetto vocal line. It's Jan's playing that makes the piece, though – with a few flourishes here and there, but perfectly pitched to let the glorious melody do the work. The piece might have ended at 2.45 as it slows to a stop, but the 'false ending' is a masterstroke, allowing a superb repeat of the introduction to fade out, with added guitar embellishments.

As a single, the song got to an amazing number four in the UK and nine in Holland. It also performed creditably in Germany and the USA.

'Carnival Fugue' (van Leer)

Here we have another stark change in tone, with a third Thijs-composed piece, this time based around the idea of a fugue, defined as (sayeth Wikipedia) a contrapuntal compositional technique in two or more voices, built on a subject (a musical theme) that is introduced at the beginning in imitation (repetition at different pitches) and which frequently recurs in the course of the composition. We begin with a stately piano with added percussion rolls and occasional guitar runs, low in the mix.

The 'fuguing' then starts in earnest, with the theme played variously on piano, acoustic guitar and bass. Again, this is intriguing stuff, requiring some attention from the listener, before the band come together in unison, Jan switching to his trusty Les Paul for a jazzier section, which develops the promised 'carnival' character as Thijs now dominates with some janty, teasing organ and piccolo before Jan enters with various layered guitar lines. When he 'solos' towards the end, there are at least three guitars overdubbed, in fact. Even at six minutes, the track, if anything, feels too short. It's another exceptional piece of music.

'Focus III' (van Leer)

This third 'episode' in the Focus saga is another one for the ages. Played at almost every Focus concert since it was released, the band often use it as an opener. This, as much as anything, is due to its qualities as a slow-build, easer-in at a Focus concert. Thijs and Jan are equals, here, with the organ line and refrain crucial, while Jan's subtle, warm guitar carries the main melody line. However, unlike 'Sylvia', he is here allowed far more room to embellish. In particular, the track is a masterclass in volume control and let us not forget that Jan used the volume knob on his Les Paul rather than a pedal. This track is all about a gradual and masterful increase in the intensity of the whole arrangement, with both Pierre and Bert crucial. When the final 'release' arrives, it is euphoric. Dropping away to silence after three minutes, the piece then repeats in its entirety but with subtle variations, particularly from Jan's guitar and this time move straight into:

'Answers? Questions! Questions? Answers!' (Ruiter, Akkerman)

We now come to the first piece to rely on lengthy sections of soloing and improvisation, and it is allowed thirteen minutes to do so. The foundation of the track is Bert's excellent riff – introduced on bass, of course, with swirls of organ and Jan's bluesy guitar line. Within a few moments, we are into the first solo – this time from Thijs on organ, with Jan providing some choppy guitar. However, this is heavily structured because we are soon back into Bert's unison riff, which this time introduces a terrific short solo from Jan, before another – different – unison section, heralds slower, bluesier – but still short – solos from guitar and organ.

The first main solo is from flute – here played behind the beat with some subtle echo to give it a slightly distant, even melancholic feel, with the band (including Thijs organ) vamping and gradually building in intensity as the solo (which is four minutes long) does the same. The flute fades away, to be replaced by Jan's guitar, again building in intensity with the rest of the band. This comes to a sudden halt after three minutes, fading away into a passage featuring more masterful volume control and a final burst of guitar as the piece drifts to an end.

Clearly recorded live in the studio except (one suspects) Thijs' flute solo, few pieces sound as 'live' as this one, with the band finishing together. You can almost feel them intuiting each other's playing. The piece works on record because the flute and guitar solos, while long, are tightly structured. In short, the track doesn't outstay its welcome despite its length, and it bears repeated listens.

'Anonymus II' (Part One) / 'Anonymus II' (Conclusion) (van Leer, Akkerman, Ruiter, van der Linden)

Masterpiece or white elephant? The world remains split on this one, with – as you will already have read – my own view squarely in the latter camp. Take a previously recorded track and adapt it with better-quality musicians to let them stretch themselves, was the thinking. There's nothing wrong with that, and to me, this merely suggests ambition rather than a surfeit of ego. Rest assured that the track is expertly structured and brilliantly played. The real question is – how often might the listener want to hear it?

We open with a tight, brilliantly played and superfast full-band version of the 'Anonymus' theme. Then, over the familiar riff from the version on the first album, we are straight into a flute solo. It's an aggressive one, this time, deliberately overblown in Ian Anderson style. As you might expect, the band are far from maintaining a 'holding pattern' while Thijs plays – with Jan chugging away impressively. The solo is then taken up by the organ before the band play in unison with a descending and ascending figure, suggesting 'Hocus Pocus' before a return to the main riff brings things to a momentary halt.

Yes, it's bass solo time. Bert plays around a little with something similar to the 'Answers? Questions! Questions? Answers!' riff, before gradually building in intensity with the occasional chug from Jan, then from Pierre and finally Thijs on organ. At this point, the band are playing a fully-fledged unison riff, allowing Jan to take up the solo, which he does in thrilling style in a searing, but very long, solo. A reprise of the main riff (at which point the vinyl and *Focus 50 Years Anthology* version fades out) leads into – you guessed it – a drum solo. It's expertly played, as you might expect, but – well – it's a drum solo, and it doesn't fit in with the 'narrative' of piece as Pierre's solo did on Eruption'. The band rejoins for another super-fast reiteration of the 'Anonymus' Theme, finishing with a more stately version with Jan soloing beautifully in both and a final – playful – fast version.

A shorter version of this piece might have worked better, with bass and drum solos removed and the other solos more tightly structured, but what would have separated that from the version of the debut, bar better playing and recording? There are no rules to say that a band can't have a second attempt at one of their pieces, after all, but – in short – this version just feels too self-indulgent, despite many thrilling moments.

'Elspeth Of Nottingham' (Akkerman)
Placed on side four of the vinyl version of the album as a defacto album closer, this charming piece summons up a pastoral world of the medieval countryside – aided by the sound of chirping birds and cows mooing. It's Jan's first foray onto the lute on a Focus album, and the accompaniments are just Thijs' recorder and Pierre's simple drum pattern. It's short but

utterly delightful. Mike Vernon came up with the title, and eagle-eared listeners will note that the lute part is an adaptation of 'Minstral' from Jan's *Profile* album, recorded two years before. In my 'fantasy single-album version' of the record, I'd have this acting at the first track.

Growing The Fanbase

Having recorded the album, the band played the Reading Festival in mid-August, although there was a frantic panic getting the band's gear – stranded in Belgium – to the festival in time, and once onstage, Jan was given an electric shock by rain dripping onto the stage from above. Ah, rock and roll in the early 70s! The band were a sensation, but the whole affair, which also included a run-in with other technicians over Focus' volume, led to a change in crew, and Jacob 'Cocky' Akkerman was replaced as the band's sound engineer. A bit like Martijn Dresden – and Jan's brother, let us not forget – Cocky never quite recovered from this humiliation, his life hitting the skids. He died in 1996, aged 43.

Following another barnstorming appearance at the *Melody Maker* Poll Winner's concert at the Oval Cricket Ground on September 30, alongside Wishbone Ash, Jack Bruce and headliners Emerson, Lake and Palmer, the band continued their progress in the UK with a further college-circuit tour – 31 gigs in 36 days – in October and November. Another poll success followed, with readers of *The New Musical Express* voting the band 'Best New Group / Promising Artist'. However, the band's real triumph was yet to come.

Focus were booked for a second appearance on *The Old Grey Whistle Test*, to be broadcast on Tuesday 12 December 1972 at 10.35 pm. By now, the show was presented by 'Whispering' Bob Harris, and in the studio, the band recorded several takes of 'Anonymus II', 'Sylvia' and 'Hocus Pocus' (with the latter two pieces segueing one to another). Quite why the band became such a sensation this time out is not clear, but it's obvious from the footage – now available on the *Focus 50 Years Anthology* – that the band are on sensational form. Not only is Jan at the top of his game, exuding virtuosity, bit there's a melodicism and romanticism about the music that is completely unlike anything else around at the time. Add to that Thijs' natural showmanship and undoubted warmth – he wishes the audience a 'Merry Christmas and a Happy New Year' during 'Hocus Pocus' – and you have a winning formula.

However, despite the undoubted success of the appearance, the often-cited sudden leap in record sales that the band experienced as a result of it appears to be a myth. On release, *Focus 3* made a single appearance in the top 50 before dropping out again, as probably befits a band of 'up and coming' stature that were on tour in the country at the time. But we'll come to that story shortly.

Profile – Jan Akkerman (Recorded 1970-1971)

Personnel:
Jan Akkerman: electric guitar, classical guitar, bass, lute, electric piano
Bert Ruiter: bass
Jaap van Eyck: bass
Frans Smit: drums
Pierre van der Linden: drums
Ferry Maat: piano
Produced by Tim Griek
Released October 1972
Highest chart places: Did not chart
Current edition: Remastered CD as part of Complete *Jan Akkerman* box set, Wounded Bird CD or Universal double CD with *Talent For Sale*

Whereas, for all its faults, Thijs' *Introspection* album, also released in 1972, had some real artistic motivation behind it, it seems very likely that releasing this album by Jan in October 1972 – having been recorded (mainly) a couple of years earlier in 1970 – was a means of cashing in, if not by Jan himself, but by his record company. This is clearly not the album Jan wanted to release – that was to come with *Tabernakel* – and the whole thing feels unfinished. Ideas are begun but not completed, and some tracks – like the excellent 'Blue Boy' – fade out much too quickly, presumably because the track was never completed properly. Jan agreed with this assessment, begging the label not to release the album.

Side one – the nineteen minute 'Fresh Air' – is the sort of piece that presents a certain fascination on first listen (a bit like the improvised section of King Crimson's 'Moonchild') but doesn't bear repeated listens, while side two – containing seven tracks in all – has some excellent material, but is far too patchy. It just feels like a bunch of disparate pieces thrown together. Which is what it is.

Nonetheless, it's a very interesting snapshot of the different styles that Jan was capable of at the very start of the Focus era. Whether a Focus fan would want to hear more than a few tracks more than once is another matter.

'Fresh Air' (Akkerman)
a. 'Must Be My Land' b. 'Wrestling To Get Out c. 'Back Again' d. 'The Fight' e. 'Fresh Air – Blue Notes For Listening' f. 'Water And Skies Are Telling Me' g. 'Happy Gabriël?'

For those that love only the lush, lyrical side of Focus, this opening nineteen-minute piece might be somewhat tortuous. Beginning with a little seemingly aimless vamping on Fender Rhodes from Jan, with drums by Pierre van der Linden, the piece them embarks on what feels like an extensive improvisation, with Bert Ruiter on bass. Beginning with a typical, choppy rhythm guitar, we hear two guitars – one soloing, while the other plays wilder, more discordant – and indeed distorted – patterns. Occasionally, this guitar breaks into soloing with the cleaner-sounding one takes a back seat, and just occasionally, there are moments of unison, not unlike 'Eruption', which help root the music.

About twelve minutes in, the other instruments fade away, and Jan solos. It's clear that he's just 'trying stuff' here, and some of his fretboards runs work while others don't. However, from here on, the piece takes on a rather more ambient, and to these ears more successful, style. Jan's heavily echoed guitars establish more of a 'Pink Floyd' tone, building gradually with some excellent bass work (possibly Jan himself), leading into a more discordant, but equally impressive section, and Jan's final solo – over two rhythm guitars – is searing, the piece finishing on a cacophony of sound.

This is all well and good; it's very much 'of its time' and very freeform. What it really lacks is any sort of discipline. One suspects it was fun to play, but – if I'm honest – it's much less fun to listen to. It does accede to Jan's love of improvisation, but this feels almost like a first draft (despite the overdubbed guitars) and doesn't really have the required structure. In short, like many improvisations, it's interesting to listen to once, but it's never going to be in anyone's top ten side-long pieces.

'Kemp's Jig' (Anonymus)
Demonstrating that he was already well developed as a lute player, this jaunty and pleasing piece kicks off side two in fine style. It's only a minute and a half long, but it's probably the best realised and most successful track on the album. This traditional piece was also recorded by the medieval rock band Gryphon, in 1973.

'Etude' (Matteo Carcassi)

Another very short piece, this time written by late 18th / early 19th Century Italian guitar virtuoso Matteo Carcassi. This shows off Jan's prowess as a classical guitarist, and again it's beautifully played.

'Blue Boy' (Akkerman)

There's a complete change of tone this time, with this wonderful full band piece. It might have been developed into a great Focus tune, and certain parts are wonderful, but it feels unfinished, fading out (before it even hits three minutes) just as it's getting going. It's frustrating – this piece has a huge amount of potential, but it's not realised. It needs – dare I say it – a touch of the van Leer fairy dust.

'Andante Sostenuto' (Anton Diabelli)

This is another somewhat obscure classical guitar piece, this time from Austrian composer Anton Diabelli. Although written in the same era that Carcassi was active, this is a longer and rather more stately piece, and while pretty enough, at over four minutes, it rather overstays it's welcome.

'Maybe Just A Dream' (Akkerman)

This is another full band piece, albeit a light and fluffy one, with Jan in pseudo-country mode. His control of the volume knob is, of course, legendary and here he shows off that skill, with accompaniment from an acoustic guitar. Again, the piece has a lovely melody, and Pierre's drumming is nicely dynamic, but it's another slight, underdeveloped track, also very much in the Focus style.

'Minstrel / Farmer's Dance' (Akkerman)

Now we have another lute piece, this time written by Jan. Sharp-eared listeners will note that the 'Minstrel' section was reworked in 1972 as 'Elspeth Of Nottingham' on *Focus 3*. The 'dance' section is also terrific but – again – frustratingly short.

'Stick' (Akkerman)

According to Peet Johnson, pianist Ferry Maat recalls a long session in the Autumn of 1970 recording pieces for Jan's proposed double solo album. This was a throwaway blues-rock number recorded at the end of the session and the only piece from said session to make the cut onto the finished album. It's sprightly and beautifully played, of course, but has 'filler' written all over it, making it a disappointing end to an interesting but deeply frustrating side of music.

'Hocus Pocus' (US Single Version, AKA Fast Version) (van Leer, Akkerman)

Personnel:

Jan Akkerman: guitars

Thijs van Leer: keyboards, flute, vocals

Bert Ruiter: bass

Pierre van der Linden: drums

Produced by Mike Vernon

Recorded by Dave Grinsted at Chipping Norton Studios, 13 December 1972

Highest chart places: Netherlands: 12, UK: 20, US: 9

Available as part of the *Focus 50 Years Anthology* and on all versions of *Hocus Pocus – The Best Of Focus*

This retread was recorded in a hurry in December 1972 at the behest of the record company, who wanted a shorter, simpler version of the piece for the US market specifically. This take has Bert on bass, although Jan has claimed that he played the bass as he did on the original. This seems to make little sense, though, particularly as the track starts – rather mischievously – with a short jam before launching into a lightning-fast version of the song. Most of the more famous 'moments' are included – there's plenty of yodelling and fast soloing – but the quirkier moments from the long version are missed out and there's no flute. Thirty seconds from the end, the piece 'breaks down' into a funky bass riff and short guitar solo into the fade-out. It's brilliantly played, but rather an odd arrangement. Considering it's relatively brief running time, it wastes precious seconds at the start and the end in what could, instead, have included more bonkers Hocus Pocusyness. But it does the job and seems to have become the accepted version when the piece is used on TV and in film.

The *Focus 50 Years Anthology* box set has a few takes of this track (14 to 17!) as a nice bonus. This gives added credence to the idea that the band played the backing tracks live in the studio and that Bert is all present and correct, playing the bass rather than Jan. The first two takes have the short jam at the start and show the band struggling to get the cue into the fast riff right. In the last two, they nail it, and in the final version, we get a complete version with Thijs' yodelling and super-fast guitar solo – both obviously overdubbed – in all their glory.

1973 – Focus Mania

The singles charts in the UK at the beginning of 1973 were strangely eclectic. They had not yet sunk into the mid-70s slump, which partially created the right environment for punk. A mixture of soul, teenybopper and glam rock songs dominated. 'Long Haired Lover From Liverpool' by Little Jimmy Osmond had been number one over Christmas 1972 and was to give way to 'Blockbuster' by The Sweet, with its riff stolen from David Bowie. 'Cum On Feel The Noize' by Slade was to follow.

The album charts – having been dominated by compilations over the Christmas period – were then taken over by albums by Slade (again) and singer-songwriters like Elton John, Carly Simon and Gilbert O'Sullivan.

It was into this environment that Focus had their greatest chart triumph outside of the Netherlands, with an astonishing run of success throughout January, February and March. As mentioned, following the band's appearance on the *Old Grey Whistle Test* in December 1972, the new album that they were promoting – *Focus 3* of course – made a single appearance in the UK chart at the start of the month at number 50. It wasn't until January when both 'Hocus Pocus' and 'Sylvia' began receiving extensive airplay that the band's fortunes really took off. And when they did, the success was sudden – and astonishing.

'Hocus Pocus' entered the chart on 14 January at a modest 40, and both albums charted in the following week – *Moving Waves* at 36 and *Focus 3* at 39. 'Sylvia' also charted that week at number 34. The following weeks saw all four platters take on lives of their own. 'Hocus Pocus' – the slouch of the bunch – peaked at number twenty on 18 February before drifting down and out in March. 'Sylvia' peaked at number four in the same week and spent four weeks in the top ten. *Focus 3* pealed at number six on 10 March, spending sixteen weeks on the chart in total. *Moving Waves* was the biggest success, however, peaking at an astonishing number two on 17 March and remaining on the chart for an astonishing 34 weeks, off and on, not leaving until August.

Two questions remain unanswered. Why did 'Sylvia' do so much better than 'Hocus Pocus'? This is probably down to its melodicism. Its structure and tune were better suited to radio play and was more able to appeal to older listeners, who were a significant proportion of singles buyers at the time. The edit of 'Hocus Pocus', which was released, was both hard rocking and unusually structured. Less obviously 'commercial' to record buyers weaned on bubblegum pop and melodic instrumentals like 'Albatross'.

Secondly, why did *Moving Waves* outperform *Focus 3?* In this writer's opinion, it's a better album, of course, but the reason is probably more pragmatic. As a double album, *Focus 3* was more expensive and given how successful both more at the same time, if a buyer had to choose, they were probably more likely to go for the single platter.

Focus Live At The BBC 1973

Personnel:
Jan Akkerman: guitars
Thijs van Leer: organ, electric piano, flute, vocals
Bert Ruiter: bass, vocals
Pierre van der Linden: drums
Produced and recorded by Jeff Griffin for BBC Radio One In Concert, Paris Theatre, London 17 January 1973.
Mastered by Wouter Bessels

Another factor in the success of Focus in the UK was a live appearance on BBC radio at the end of January, as part of their headlining UK tour (which helped propel them into the charts). The one hour concert was recorded at The Paris Theatre in London on 17 January and broadcast ten days later. It now appears as the eighth CD on the *Focus 50 Years Anthology* and while it contains a similar set to *At The Rainbow*, 'Eruption' is replaced by 'Focus 1' and a 23-minute 'Anonymus II'. The main reason for seeking this out is quite simple. The band are simply on fire, and – despite the introductions from the silver-voiced Bob Harris – this is a much better representation of the band at their fiery best than the 'official' live show recorded by a slightly more jaded band in May. While I am no great lover of 'Anonymus II', this is a far better version than the somewhat flabby studio rendition, with its solos – especially Ruiter's – getting to the point rather earlier. Although it's too close to *At The Rainbow* to review track by track without pointless repetition, I urge all Focus fans to seek this out. You won't get a better live representation of the band at the height of its powers than this.

At The Rainbow – Live Album

Personnel:
Jan Akkerman: guitars
Thijs van Leer: organ, electric piano, flute, vocals
Bert Ruiter: bass, vocals

Pierre van der Linden: drums
Produced by Mike Vernon
Recorded by Phil Dunne using the Pye Studios Mobile Unit at the Rainbow Theatre,
London, May 5 1973
Mixed by John Punter and Gareth Edwards at Air Studios, London
Highest chart places: Netherlands: 9, UK: 23, US: 135
Available as part of the *Focus 50 Years Anthology* or Red Bullet CD

From the end of February until April, the band set their sights on the USA,
where a staggered release for Focus II / Moving Waves and Focus 3 and a
top ten hit in 'Hocus Pocus' made them almost as big a prospect in the
USA as they had been in the UK. The band returned home later in the
spring, playing in the Netherlands and then back for another jaunt around
the UK, where they were to record their first official live album.

Live albums are often stop-gap measures, recorded at the height of a
bands popularity to give the public something to chew on while new
material is being prepared. This is definitely the case here, with the band
riding a wave of success due to the singles performance of 'Sylvia' and
two chart albums. Recorded hastily on the Pye Mobile unit at the Rainbow
Theatre in London in early May 1973, this is a decent – if somewhat
truncated – representation of the band's then-current set. There are no
surprises with all the material taken from *Focus 3* and *Focus II / Moving
Waves*. It's absolutely fine, and there are a few interesting variations for the
purists, but as live albums go, it's hardly essential. Mike Vernon's mixing of
what is also a high-quality recording has to be praised. It certainly sounds
better than other contemporary live albums by other bands likethe Yes
triple-live album *Yessongs,* and it sounds authentic, too. No overdubs.

The issue of whether the album should have been a double album also
rears its head. Was the band's set long enough? Given that it was recorded
on one night, on May 5th, it could be that the performances weren't up to
snuff or that the record company wanted to keep costs down and release
a single album. As a result, the album feels a little throwaway, despite an
expensive cover design for initial pressings.

'Focus III' (van Leer)
A brief announcement and then Thijs' organ opens the set with their
standard opener at the time. Clearly, the audience know their stuff, as the
applause of recognition demonstrates. Jan adds plenty of light and shade
to his interpretation, delaying his entry until the last possible moment.

The rest of the band are excellent, with Bert pleasingly high in the mix and Thijs adds a little falsetto vocalising. It's a shortened version of the piece, but none the worse for it.

'Answers? Questions! Questions? Answers!' (Akkerman, Ruiter)

Thijs adds more vocalisations in the bridge between the two songs, and the whole piece shows a noticeable increase in pace and intensity from the album version. Both organ and guitar solos are taken at frightening power, while the bluesier solo after the tempo change is also superb. The control of pace and subtlety from the entire band, especially the rhythm section, is astonishing, particularly during Thijs' flute solo. Jan is noticeably out of tune towards the end of this section (that's live music for you), but his next solo, when it comes, is superbly constructed and builds while the other three members ramp up their accompaniment to match the intensity of this playing. This final solo – which closes the piece – is a four-minute tour de force.

'Focus II' (van Leer)

A short new organ introduction heralds this, the greatest of short Focus pieces. There are some interesting variations here, too, for sharp-eared listeners. The warmth of Jan's guitar compared with the original is dialled down a little, and some of the faster sections are taken at a smarter, rather more military tempo. But it's still a fine rendition.

'Eruption' (van Leer, Barlache)

Thijs announces the previous three pieces, then goes on to introduce a truncated version of the band's side-long masterpiece from *Focus II / Moving Waves*. Again, there's a noticeable increase in energy in this version, with the 'Answer' sections taken at one hell of a pace. The second 'Orfeus' features a new melody played on Jan's volume-controlled guitar and the second 'Answer' has a nicely harmonised duet between organ and guitar as it segues into 'Pupilla'. 'Tommy' is the perfect showcase for Jan, and he doesn't disappoint, with just enough variation to excite, but not so much that it jars, and a final 'Pupilla' brings the piece – slightly disappointingly – to a close. There's a real whiff of an edit here, and the audience applause feels tacked on, so one suspects that the band played more of the piece than we get here, which is a disappointment.

'Hocus Pocus' (van Leer, Akkerman)

From some pieces early in the set, we're now in the encores (or perhaps the final piece of the main set) by the sounds of it, with this extended version of 'Hocus Pocus'. After some vamping from Jan, we're into a lightening-fast version of this famous piece with Pierre and Bert playing at full tilt. There's more emphasis on yodelling here, with Jan's guitar also, of course, prominent. Four minutes in, the track gets an extra dose of energy before some variations, including an extended yodel from Thijs, which heralds audience applause and a whistling section. We also get the obligatory band introductions, half-spoken and half-sung by Thijs, and a playful 'rock and roll' ending. It's a crowd-pleasing rendition, which was probably more impressive in a live setting than it is or record, excellent though it is.

'Sylvia' (van Leer)

The band have obviously been offstage, as the rhythmic applause testifies. Some more choppy vamping from Jan introduces 'the hit' (in the UK at least) and it's another high energy and beautifully played version, despite a slight mistake from Jan. It leads into:

'Hocus Pocus (Reprise)' (van Leer, Akkerman)

A further snatch of 'the other hit' finishes off the set in fine style. It includes an entertaining falsetto section from Thijs, building into a final salvo of the main riff played even faster than before. A final burst of audience applause and it's all over.

Two Sides Of Peter Banks

Personnel:
Peter Banks: acoustic guitar, synthesizer, electric piano
Jan Akkerman: acoustic guitar, electric guitar
Ray Bennett: bass
Phil Collins: drums
Produced by Peter Banks
Recorded at Advision Studios, London, between November 1972 and June 1973
Highest chart places: did not chart
Currently unavailable on CD, but available on streaming services

Given that this was a hugely busy time for Focus, Jan made another significant recorded appearance in 1973, this time on Flash guitarist Peter

Banks' debut solo album, *Two Sides Of Peter Banks*. There is a certain irony in this, considering that it was the former Yes guitarist's much more extravagant stagecraft that is sometimes cited as a cause of management dissatisfaction with Jan's presence in Brainbox back in 1969. Nonetheless, the two musicians – who met when Flash opened for Focus in Holland in 1972 – developed a friendship and a creative relationship. Banks, who sadly died in 2013, wrote about this collaboration in his 2001 memoir *Beyond And Before:*

> I eventually booked some time with Advision Studios one evening after a gig, about 1:00 in the morning. Jan and I just set up our equipment in this very small room, with his Marshall in one corner, and mine in the other corner. We then proceeded to kind of play at each other — sometimes at deafening volume. These jams were recorded and then scrupulously edited for my solo album. I think the length of the original tapes of Jan and I jamming were around four hours. And of course, it was total free-form playing; obviously nothing was discussed. The tape operator had literally nothing to do, and we had to wake him up to change the reels. These jams were recorded on a two-track fifteen-inch reel-to-reel. They were then transferred to 24-track. And this material turned out to be the basis for side two of my solo album…

In the end, while Banks was happy with what he'd created, and although the reviews were quite decent, Jan was typically critical of the final result:

> Jan Akkerman was not happy with the album at all. But then again, he's not easily pleased. Even though Jan actually plays a lot better than I do on it, I was happy about that. In a lot of the stuff on my album, I'm following Jan — he takes the lead on a lot of it. I remember when the album was finished, and I played it for him. Jan said, 'It's terrible — you can't release it like this! Why did you put this piece on it?' and 'Why did you put that on it?' It was all that kind of thing. I know his management were kind of tough on the deal, and I believe we split it 50/50 on the publishing. But there was absolutely no enthusiasm from Jan Akkerman about my album at all — he hated it.

It seems likely that the session with Jan was recorded at Advison in November 1972, when Focus were on tour in the UK. Jan is on six tracks in total, so we'll look at these in a little detail.

'Vision Of The King' (Akkerman, Banks)

This is a short introductory piece, of ambient intent, with Jan leading an impressive exercise in volume control and Banks following. While it does sound improvised, as you might expect, Banks' is impressive in the way that he compliments Jan's playing. It's a promising start.

'Battles' (Akkerman, Banks)

Jan next appears after the lengthy 'White House Vale' suite, in another short and jammy piece with Jan laying down a funky rhythm that Banks solos over. Phil Collins' drumming on this piece is particularly impressive, considering that he probably recorded after the guitars were laid down.

'Last Eclipse' (Akkerman, Banks)

Another quiet, ambient piece closes the first side of the album. Given that the notes come in a rather stately and controlled way, it's not quite clear who is playing what, though so skilled is the volume control once again that the lead instrument is probably Jan's with Banks' providing back up.

'Beyond The Loneliest Sea' (Akkerman)

We switch to acoustic instruments for this flamenco-inspired piece, whose only writing credit goes to Jan. His acoustic guitar is the star, and it's a performance of wonderful virtuosity and dexterity. After a Jan-only introduction, it sounds like Banks dubbed on guitar and some keyboards later. Jan was almost certainly improvising, and so the added instrumentation – mainly Fender Rhodes scales and some volume control lead guitar from Banks – doesn't quite hang together, but it's still a charming listen.

'Stop That!' (Akkerman, Banks)

The longest piece on the album fades in, and we feel like we are arriving during the middle of a jam. Which indeed we are. Phil Collins again provides drums – marvellously sensitive and jazzily played – while Ray Bennett of Flash contributes some rather nicely performed bass, with Banks dubbing on some Fender Rhodes later. That said, this feels like one of the improvised pieces on *Profile*. It must have been fun to play, and the performances from both musicians are good, particularly when their lead lines weave around each other, and Jan's soloing, in particular, is astonishing. Banks throws in a familiar nursery rhyme motif at the start of a solo – a familiar trope of his. It does ebb and flow impressively, and the rhythm section have done a good job in interpreting those shifts in tempo after the event. However, it's hugely self-indulgent, so why anyone would really want to listen to this piece more than once or twice is a mystery.

'Get Out Of My Fridge' (Akkerman, Banks)

Ah, a Country Jam for finish on! It's good fun and very different in tone to the rest of the album, but, again, it's two good guitarists doing their best to compete with each other, while the rhythm section tries to keep up. It's either a jolly album closer, with mistakes aplenty, or a bit of a mess, depending on which interpretation you prefer.

Chipping *Where*?

The history of rock music is littered by incidences of the story that comes next. A band becomes suddenly successful and tours widely – and gruellingly – over a lengthy period. They are then rushed into a studio to record their next album without the opportunity adequately to develop new material and exhausted after their live endeavours. Some bands thrive on the pressure this produces, of course. But not Focus.

The band's UK tour finished on 17 May at Fairfield halls in Croydon, a lovely venue with great acoustics, and without any sort of break at all – they did not return home to the Netherlands. Instead, they headed 75 miles West to the town of Chipping Norton in Oxfordshire to begin work on the next album. The studio there was owned by Mike Vernon and his brother Richard, and on the face of it, it seemed like a decent location. Chipping Norton is very much part of a farming community and is a quiet and pleasant town, with little distractions except for a few pubs. It must have seemed the ideal location for the new album.

However, the band did not feel the same way. Tensions on the road had taken their toll. Jan preferred to see the surrounding countryside or to stay in his hotel room, choosing to work – when he did – at nights, while Thijs, Pierre and Bert worked as a unit during the day. Furthermore, Pierre felt that he was drifting apart from Jan musically and – having supposedly been asked to simplify his playing approach on one of the new pieces – was suffering from a crisis of confidence. He became withdrawn and difficult to communicate with.

The material that has survived does suggest that the band were not quite in the right frame of mind to produce their best work. Only 'P's March' was considered finished and good enough to release at the time, although the delightful – if brief – 'Focus V' is another highlight. It's clear that the long-form piece 'Vesuvius' wasn't working and other pieces reveal more about the mental state of Jan and Pierre than they do about the band as a whole.

With the band due to head to the USA and Canada for the summer touring circuit, Vernon was forced to abandon the sessions. It was not a happy time. However, the shows in North America gave the band the opportunity to perform alongside a huge host of major acts. Their support for part of the tour were fusion band Return To Forever, a group with jazz credentials who were dipping their toes into the rock world. It seems that Thijs and now-legendary keys man Chic Corea (who died in February 2021) developed a considerable bond during this leg. The 'festivals' segment of the tour – the summer festival circuit was, and remains, a huge part of the North American live music experience – would see many European bands such as Yes, Deep Purple, Emerson, Lake and Palmer and Jethro Tull disappearing into this huge country for months on end. By this time, Focus were a big live draw and they played a full part in that 1973 season.

The Chipping Norton Sessions (as they appear on Ship Of Memories)

Personnel:
Jan Akkerman: guitars, rhythm box
Thijs van Leer: organ, electric piano, flute, vocals
Bert Ruiter: bass
Pierre van der Linden: drums
Produced by Mike Vernon at Chipping Norton Studios, May 1973
Mixed and mastered by Mike Vernon and Barry Hammond at Chipping Norton Studios, September 1976
Currently available as part of Ship Of Memories as part of the Focus 50 Years Anthology box set or on Red Bullet CD

'P's March' (van Leer)

This jaunty, folky tune was considered to be the only track good enough for possible release at the time and was earmarked as a single. It's a showcase for Thijs' various woodwinds, in the main, with Jan providing solid, hard-rocking support. A minute and a half in, there's a change in tone as Jan plays a typically lyrical lead line, with both organ and Mellotron providing support, before a brief return to the main theme. This is followed by another guitar solo which seems lacking in inspiration, despite a nice moment where the guitar seems to 'laugh'. Structurally, it's an odd piece. The main melody is very strong, though a touch repetitive, but the 'Jan' sections are not particularly convincing. He doesn't quite sound 'into' what he's playing, and one suspects a few more takes – had Jan been willing to attempt them – might have produced better results. So, it's a strong enough opening, but not quite up with the band's best.

'P's March' was mixed in July 1973 and was intended as a single in October 1973. It was shelved in favour of *At The Rainbow* as there would have been no studio album to follow it, and this mix and a single edit are available in the *Focus 50 Years Anthology* Box. This decision not to release the single was questionable. Despite the band's high profile at the time, live albums are always, at best, a stop-gap and another hit single might have kept the momentum going in the UK. As it was, this momentum was partially lost.

'Can't Believe My Eyes' (Akkerman)

According to Vernon's sleeve notes, this bizarre piece was originally called 'Can't Believe My Ears' before later being re-titled (somewhat more appropriately) 'Dance Macabre'. Recorded early on in the Chipping Norton sessions, it's effectively a five-minute guitar solo with a rather sinister Mellotron backing. We feel like we are arriving in the middle of some demonic ritual, and while Pierre sounds like he's enjoying what he's doing, it takes Bert a while to find his way into the piece, and his bass playing gains confidence as it progresses. But this is Jan's track and he sounds completely committed here, albeit hardly in a happy frame of mind, although there's a real feel of 'let's try this and see where it goes' about it. The piece abounds with eerie noises and discordant, distorted guitars. Thijs stops playing completely about a minute from the end, and the track ends with a couple of somewhat disjointed coda's. As a piece in its own right, it's a tough listen, to be honest. I could see this working as a short subsection of a longer piece, but on its own, it's rather unpleasant in tone and far from finished.

'Focus V' (van Leer)

This is, without doubt, the standout piece of the existing sessions and fully deserving of its place amongst the 'Focus' sequence of tracks. It was one of the tracks that it was hard to get Jan out of his Oxfordshire hotel to record. He finally recorded the guitar part late one night, and what a triumph it is. His playing is so far behind the beat that it almost feels 'lazy'. However, this is just what is required for the piece, and when Thijs' flute enters just after the halfway mark, it feels like they are in the same room together. Which they almost certainly weren't. When Jan's guitar re-enters, he compliments the lush Mellotron accompaniment beautifully, while Bert and Pierre should also be complimented for some fabulously restrained and subtle playing. If the piece has a fault, it is simply that it is too short! It could certainly have taken another section or element. But this is splitting hairs – it's a gorgeous track.

'Out Of Vesuvius' (van Leer, Akkerman, Ruiter, van der Linden)
Side one of *Ship Of Memories* ends with the final substantive piece from the Chipping Norton sessions, and this is a section of the side-long piece the band were working on before the sessions were abandoned. Again, it's something of a jam, if rather easier on the ear than 'Can't Believe My Eyes'. Once again, Jan dominates, with a bluesy solo, with both Bert and Pierre sounding at home on such familiar territory, while Thijs accompanies on electric piano. Jan sounds great here; his playing is bluesy but also well thought out and committed. Thijs takes over with an electric piano later in the piece, while Jan chugs away in typical style before we fade out. The problem is that while it's a fragment, it's a long one and one can imagine that it would have been edited and honed into something more accessible for the final album. As it is, it feels like the sort of improvisation the band might have played in concert, and it's not unlike some of their work in *Focus 3*. It's interesting as a work in progress, but as a listen in its own right, the track sounds far from finished.

'Glider' (Akkerman)
For many years, there was some doubt over the chronology of this piece, as Vernon suggests that it might have been recorded in Brussels around 1975, yet Thijs van Leer suggested to Peet Johnson that it was recorded at Chipping Norton in 1973. You'd have thought Vernon would remember, though, and the tune – which would later reappear in amended and smoothed out form on *Mother Focus* as the title track – doesn't really have much in common with the Chipping Norton sessions, particularly Pierre's drum sound and Jan's guitar. In fact, this feels like an attempt at a single, with Thijs' yodelling and his other crowd-pleasing vocal mannerisms.

However, Focus and Jan Akkerman archivist Wouter Bessels seems to have cleared up the provenance of this track once and for all, placing it very much as a 1973 recording, albeit with a very different tone to the other pieces recorded during that time.

Despite its relative lack of polish, this version does have a certain charm. It develops out of a brief jam against a rhythm box backing. It's a slightly faster take on the piece and genuinely benefits from some excellent lead guitar from Jan, plus a winning riff which is played on both piano and electric sitar. It loses its way slightly in the last minute or so, as it just repeats the riff on piano while Jan solos, but it's still rather good and certainly more dynamic than the version they were to record a couple of years later.

'Ship Of Memories' (Pierre van der Linden)

Recorded right at the end of the Chipping Norton sessions, this impressionistic solo piece from Pierre is essentially a drum solo accompanied by some mournful chords played on the harmonium. As an expression of his slightly morose state of mind, it does a good job. As a piece of music, it's rather unsettling and an odd way to close the album, as it did with *Ship Of Memories*. An extended version appears as part of the *Focus 50 Years Anthology* box set.

Pierre Leaves

The tensions within the band continued, however, as 1973 continued. The band were developing in a proggier and rockier direction, which alienated Pierre, and like Jan, he disliked playing the same material night after night. He has never really recovered from the crisis he had suffered in Oxfordshire, and he was also felt ignored by audiences – finding all the attention that was being paid to Thijs and Jan difficult to deal with. The band took a short break in the Netherlands after returning from America in September, and when they reconvened at the Kasteel for further rehearsals, Pierre did not show up. Had he overslept? No – he had left the group.

In a pattern that was to be repeated at the start of 1976 when (spoiler alert) Jan left the group, there was a frantic attempt to find a big-name replacement. It is a credit to Focus' perceived stature at the time, that the drum position might even be considered by the likes of Mitch Mitchell (most famous for his place in the Jimi Hendrix Experience) and Aynsley Dunbar (of Zappa fame) – busy drummers both in terms of their playing styles and their work diaries.

Although a little further down the fame-o-meter, the final solution was former Stone The Crows member Colin Allen. The suggestion to call on Colin came from Mike Vernon, who was an old friend of the amiable Englishman, and he felt that Allen's R & B and jazz/blues background would suit the band. Although he had hardly played since the demise of his previous band, some intensive work with Thijs and Jan (separately, of course) licked him into shape in time for the next jaunt to the USA in the autumn, by which time some of the material from the next album, *Hamburger Concerto*, had made its way into the set.

Tabernakel – Jan Akkerman

Selected personnel:
Jan Akkerman: electric guitar, acoustic guitar, lute, bass, percussion, organ
Ray Lucas: drums
Tim Bogert: bass
Carmine Appice: drums
George Flynn: harpsichord, piano, glockenspiel
Orchestra and chorus conducted by George Flynn
Produced by Geoffrey Haslam
Recorded at Atlantic Recording Studios, New York
Recording Engineers: Gene Paul and Joel Kerr
Highest chart places: Did not chart
Current edition: Remastered CD as part of *Complete Jan Akkerman* box set or BGO double CD with *Eli*

It's fair to say that the Focus management were never particularly keen to see band members embark on solo projects. However, Thijs had had great success with the first *Introspection* album, and following the abortive Chipping Norton sessions in the spring of 1973, it was now Jan's turn once again. Although *Profile* had finally been released late in 1972 and had been promoted by Jan with an appearance on *The Old Grey Whistle Test*, it represented music created – in some cases – three years previously. It was more a 'trial run' than a serious statement about where Jan was musically in 1973.

Having wanted to sign Focus in 1971, Ahmet Ertegun at Atlantic agreed to release Jan's next solo album on his Atco label, and the record was recorded over an intense two week period at Atlantic Studios in New York during the summer of 1973. One important additional recruitment was composer and arranger George Flynn, who provided some crucial support with arrangements and additional compositional ideas on some of the tracks that were to become the showcase pieces of the album. This led to the use of a string section on some of the pieces, to good effect. Flynn told David Randall:

> I was working with Ilhan Mimaroglu at Atlantic then, recording my own piano music. Ilhan thought I could make some positive contributions to Jan's album. This idea was apparently agreeable to Jan, and soon we were collaborating. I found the music of Focus interesting and felt that Jan was very accomplished on the guitar as well as the lute, and had devised some imaginative improvisations that I felt I could work with.

There is no doubt that *Tabernakel* is an interesting and skilful album. Many Focus fans believe it to be Jan's finest solo album, since it most resembles that band in some ways. Tonally, however, it is all over the place, combining short pieces played on the lute with more expansive showcases, featuring rock guitar.

Jan also uses the album to showcase his love of the lute, in particular the work of John Dowland (1563 – 1626). Dowland was a lutist, singer and composer. Best known for his songs, he also composed many lute pieces, spending a great deal of time in Europe where he even carried out some espionage missions for Sir Robert Cecil. His compositions have been recorded many times in more recent years.

Given the profile that Jan enjoyed at the time, side one – which is mainly a showcase for the lute, with the slightly jarring addition of 'House Of The King' stuck in the middle – must have mystified many. Had they all featured the expansive arrangements that 'Britannia' does, then the album might have been more accessible. But five solo lute pieces on the first side alone – no matter how pleasant and worthy – must have been a bit of a stretch for a listener expecting plenty of lead Les Paul.

Indeed, George Flynn's contributions give the album a real contemporary, almost avant-garde character, which might not have been so prominent had the album been made without his contributions. This, and the solo lute pieces, give the album a very unusual tone. You have probably never heard a solo album quite like this before.

'Britannia By John Dowland' (Arranged and adapted by Jan Akkerman and George Flynn)

The first thing that stands out in this fabulous opener is just how skilled Jan is on the lute. However, it doesn't end there, and after a short initial burst of solo playing, Jan is joined by a rhythm section (including his own bass) and a beautifully arranged small orchestra, with horns especially prominent. It's all intricately arranged and performed and makes for a delightful and exuberant opening.

'Coranto For Mrs. Murcott By Francis Pilkington'
(Arranged and adapted by Jan Akkerman)
This is a short solo lute piece – somewhat more sedate than the opener – by 16th / 17th century English lute player, vocalist and composer Francis Pilkington. A coranto was an early form of newspaper or information sheet. It's not known who Mrs. Murcott was. Again, it's beautifully performed.

'The Earl Of Derby, His Galliard By John Dowland'
(Arranged and adapted by Jan Akkerman)
It's back to John Dowland for this galliard – a sort of formal athletic dance of the 16th Century during which time it was particularly loved by Elizabeth 1st. The Earl Of Derby was a prominent nobleman in the England of this era, regardless of which individual held the Earldom at any given time. Jan's performance of this short lute piece is particularly notable for the highly skilled fretboard runs towards the end.

'House Of The King' (Akkerman)
Like Thijs before him, Jan could never quite shake off the influence of Focus. This version of (arguably) his most famous composition, however, does try a few new tricks to separate itself from the version by the band. The rhythm section, here, is Bogart and Appice of Vanilla Fudge, while as well as electric guitar and electric sitar, Jan slaps a tambourine with great gusto. There hardly seems room for a string section on such a breezy piece, but it's there all the same, presumably arranged by an uncredited George Flynn. Indeed, with Jan's guitar taking the main melody line, the 'guitar break' from the Focus version is played by the violins. There's even a flute in there somewhere, playing a counter melody. Overall, it's a fun and energetic reworking of a classic track, although it's unlikely that many listeners will play it instead of its Focus counterpart.

'A Galliard By Anthonie Holborne' (Arranged and adapted by Jan Akkerman)
It's back to the solo lute for this gentle and melodic piece, written by the Elizabethan composer, lute and cittern player Holborne. Presumably, it was a slow galliard this time! A touch earlier than some of the other

composers on the album, Holborne was a major influence on Dowling, who dedicated one of his pieces to the older man.

'A Galliard By John Dowland' (Arranged and adapted by Jan Akkerman)
Another virtuoso lute performance by Jan, here, and another very short piece by Dowland.

'A Pavane By Thomas Morley' (Arranged and adapted by Jan Akkerman)
You will have seen the pavane performed in period dramas. It is a slow, processional dance most popular in the 16th and 17th centuries. Morley was another singer and organist, best known for madrigals and he was probably the most famous composer of secular music in England during the Elizabethan period. Born in Norwich, he died in 1602, but his grave was destroyed during the Great Fire Of London in 1666. Although best known for his vocal pieces, he also wrote instrumentals, of which this is one.

'Javeh' (Akkerman / Flynn)
Jan considers his Jewish roots in this lovely piece co-written with Flynn. Jan wrote the basic music while sitting on his farm in Friesland and named it 'Javeh' (The God Of Israel) as he felt the music was almost writing itself. After Flynn's input, however, there's a feeling of the contemporary classics about this, with hints of the avant-garde. Jan roots the piece in the familiar, however, with some flamenco-inspired classical guitar, while the orchestra and a solo violin weave textures around his playing. Indeed his guitar is reminiscent of 'Le Clochard' from *Focus II* / *Moving Waves*. Flynn also provides keyboards – particularly some well-placed harpsichord. It's an interesting piece, certainly, but provides another stylistic jump in a very varied – perhaps even too varied – album.

'A Fantasy By Laurencini Of Rome' (Arranged and adapted by Jan Akkerman)
A fantasy or fantasia is a wide-ranging musical style that celebrates the power of imagination, often via improvisation. This slightly longer lute piece, however, is by Italian composer Laurencini (or Lorencini).

'Lammy' (based on a musical idea by Akkerman). 1. 'I Am' (Akkerman / Flynn) 2. 'Asleep, Half Asleep, Awake' (Akkerman)

3. 'She Is' (Akkerman / Flynn) 4. 'Lammy, We Are' (Akkerman / Flynn) 5. 'The Last Will And Testament' (Holborne, Arranged and adapted by Akkerman and Flynn) 6. 'Amen' (Flynn / Akkerman) So we come to the final, fourteen-minute centrepiece of the album. Named after Jan's second wife, it's a sprawling, sometimes brilliant piece of music, completely unlike anything you are ever likely to hear within the progressive rock genre. Does it hold together as a unified piece of music? Probably not. However, it always intrigues, and the compositional skills of George Flynn once again move the music, at times, into the realm of the contemporary classics. The two avant-garde choral pieces for which Flynn was particularly responsible are especially challenging. This is particularly evident in the opening section, 'I Am', which begins with pipe organ (played by Jan) and voices, leading into an even more avant-garde section, again based around the organ and some wild percussion (played by Jan). We then enter a mystical passage, with flavours of the far east, Jan playing guitar with an almost sitar-like flavour ('Half asleep'). After a brief flurry of kit drums, the full band enter to accompany this section, Appice and Bogart laying down a funky groove over which Jan solo's on electric guitar in much more of a 'Focus' style ('Half Awake').

Chorus and organ re-emerge suddenly for the brief, acerbic 'She Is' before band and string section gives us the lyrical and melodic 'Lammy We Are' – perhaps the album's finest section, with Jan mainly contributing strummed acoustic and some electric rhythm while the strings carry the main melody. It's an interesting sequence, in fact, sweet and melodic on the surface but always threatening to descend into cacophony. Most of the instrumentation dies away to leave a few strings, flute, lute and harpsichord for the 'Last Will And Testament' section, an arrangement of another tune by Holborne. The piece ends with choral voices only and a delightful 'Amen'.

1974 – Fast Food

Following a break in December, Focus – with Colin Allen still settling in – decamped to their favoured rehearsal space – one of the big, ornate rooms at Kasteel Groenevald – to continue rehearsals for their next album, the first since Pierre's departure. It must have been chilly that January, in more ways than one. The band then moved back into Olympic B studios in Barnes to begin recording with Mike Vernon and new engineer Bob Hall.

Taking a break in February, both Thijs and Jan were invited to play selections of their solo works at the RAI Congrescentrum in Amsterdam on February 15, to be broadcast live on TV. With Roger van Otterloo slated to conduct the orchestra, Jan asked for George Flynn to be flown in for his pieces. However, rehearsals did not go well, the orchestra struggling with Flynn's adventurous, modern arrangements for 'Britannia'. As a result, Jan had to perform solo on acoustic guitar. Allegedly, however, distracted by some chatter in the orchestral pit, Jan walked off, never to return. The Dutch press had a field day. Thijs pieces, from Intropection, went off without a hitch, giving a huge boost to sales for the album. The whole incident hardly helped the fragile relationship between the two bandmates.

Hamburger Concerto

Personnel:

Jan Akkerman: electric and acoustic guitars, lute, timpani, handclaps

Thijs van Leer: organ, grand piano, harpsichord, electric piano, Minimoog, vibes, accordion, church organ, soprano flute, alto flute, recorder, handclaps, vocals

Bert Ruiter: bass, autoharp, percussion, handclaps. vocals

Colin Allen: drums, percussion, handclaps

Produced by Mike Vernon

Recorded and mixed by Bob Hall, David Hamilton-Smith and Rod Thear at Olympic Studios, Barnes, January to March 1974

Highest chart places: Netherlands: 5, UK: 20, USA: 66

Currently available as part of the *Focus 50 Years Anthology* box set or on Red Bullet CD

By the time the band reconvened at the start of January 1974, relations between Thijs and Jan were at an all-time low. The pattern from nine months previously was repeated. Colin, Bert and Thijs recorded as a group during the day, while Jan arrived later to work on his guitar parts. Of course, there must have been some collaboration, but it's fairly safe to assume that these were worked out during the rehearsal period in the Netherlands in 1973. When it came to actually laying down the album, they barely spoke.

Hamburger Concerto is an album that splits fans. For some, it is the band's finest achievement; the ultimate realisation of the heavier, more symphonic direction for which they were striving. To others, it is an album long on ambition but short on decent material. Much of your opinion about the album will be based on whether you like the side-long title track or not. Despite many, many plays over the years, I remain unconvinced about this piece. To these ears, it plods, not helped by Colin Allen's one-dimensional drumming. It's not necessarily his fault, of course. He can only play what's presented to him, after all.

A larger recording budget also meant many more 'toys' for Thijs to play with – used to varying effect. The resulting album took the band further into the territory already occupied, to huge acclaim, by Yes and Emerson Lake and Palmer in particular, whose worldwide success some members of the band and its management must have envied. There are no obvious singles on the album, however, although 'Harem Scarem' has some surface similarities to 'Hocus Pocus' and was a hit single in the Netherlands, reaching number 22. While the album performed creditably in some territories – reaching five in the Netherlands and twenty in the UK, a very modest 66 in the USA was a considerable disappointment. Had the bubble burst?

However, I do agree with those fans that consider the first side of the album to be wonderful. This really *is* Focus experimenting with a development of their own sound and doing it successfully. 'Birth', in particular, demonstrates that building a track around a single riff can work over an extended piece. If they took this too far on side two, who can blame them?

Partially as a result of this, the band and their management decided not to use Mike Vernon producer going forward. Vernon had overseen three wildly varied albums. Although his finest work is on *Focus II / Moving Waves,* his steady hand and fine interpersonal skills had held the band together through the continuing disagreements between Thijs and Jan. While the relationship between the two within the band would continue for another eighteen months, it was, in many ways, the end of an era.

The title of the album was suggested as a sort of comment about life on the road, particularly their experiences in the USA in 1973 when they ate a huge amount of fast food. Other titles considered were 'Kloten' (testicles), which was to have been a risqué comment on the band's new, beefier sound, and not a discussion of the qualities of the tunes therein (i.e. 'bollocks'). 'Trend' was also considered but rejected as the band considered themselves the antithesis of 'trendy'.

'Delitiae Musicae' (Joachim van den Hove, adapted by Jan Akkerman)

'Delightful Music' is the translation of the title of this short piece, originally written by 16th / 17th-century dutch composer and lute player Joachim van den Hove, and here adapted by Jan. The original composer is not credited on vinyl or CD versions of the album. It's the perfect opener, as if curtains are being drawn back or a book opened. As with his *Tabernakel* album, Jan is featured on the lute with Thijs accompanying on the recorder, with two recorder parts at the end of the piece. It's a rather less cerebral, and more playfully Elizabethan piece than the similar tracks on the *Tabernakel* album and makes for charming listening.

'Harem Scarem' (van Leer)

Released as a single. Highest chart places: Netherlands: 22

The album starts in earnest with this joyous piece composed by Thijs at his new home in Belgium. There are similarities, on the surface, to 'Hocus Pocus' as the ascending organ/vocal figure that is repeated a few times in the track is not dissimilar. However, Thijs pounding piano identifies this as a pastiche of boogie rather than hard rock. Thijs' heavily reverbed 'yea, yea, yeas' also demonstrate where the influences of the track come from. But that's not all; we also divert delightfully into passages of melodic lead guitar and a rather exotic-sounding accordion, as well as funky hard rock, with Jan's first use of the talkbox, albeit low in the mix. Colin's rather more straight-down-the-line drumming works here, as a solid groove is needed, rather than Pierre's jazzier flights of fantasy, while Bert comes into his own with some terrifically mobile bass, especially during Jan's funky solo section. It's a terrific opener and very 'Focus'.

'La Cathedrale De Strasbourg' (van Leer)

We now join Thijs as he reflects on his childhood visits to the magnificent cathedral in Strasbourg in France. It was not the structure itself that excited him so much as the sound of the bells. This is very much reflected in the music.

Indeed, now we have a rather different Focus, albeit a superbly impressive one. We open with dramatic piano, later accompanied by church organ and then synthesisers, as this neo-classical structure gives way to something a little more reflective. The second section of this all-keyboard, two-minute introduction actually sounds like early Toto. Were Focus an influence on David Paich and Steve Porcaro? It's very possible.

The 'main' full-band section features keyboards again, with Thijs singing in two different octaves and then whistling over the repeated 'ding, dong' motif. This is rather jazzier, and we are a full three minutes in before we hear Jan, but when we do, he really makes it count. His guitar is warm and comforting and continues in the same fashion as the piece increases in tempo. We end on multi-tracked voices as the piece slows to a gentle stop. While this is a new Focus indeed, it's also suggests a mature and confident band, experimenting with new textures. It's an ambitious and charming piece – something of an unheralded masterpiece.

'Birth' (Akkerman)

We begin in the Renaissance, as Thijs playful harpsichord gives us the 'Birth' theme for the first time. Colin then exclaims 'here we go' before introducing the main track with a roll of toms. This is a more impressionistic piece, with Jan giving the initial limelight to Thijs, who accompanies on organ, harpsichord and flute before Jan takes his first solo, which is bluesy. Unlike Thijs' more structured compositions, there is more room for improvisation here, rather in *Focus 3* style, with Thijs (flute) and then Jan taking excellent but relatively short solos. The main motif is repeated just enough – not so much that it becomes repetitive – and when the piece slows, Jan takes another great rock solo followed by another on flute from Thijs and a final one from Jan. This is Focus 'rocking out' but really making it work.

There's an argument that suggests that a faster pace might have made this track even more of a success. However, the piece 'works' because it plays to the band's strengths. Colin's drumming style is suitable for the relatively slow pace of the track but allows it to build when needed, while Thijs and Jan – almost for the first time on the album – are allowed to show off their chops as rock soloists. It's a great end to a superb first side.

Given that the *Hambuger Concerto* tour's surviving video footage does not include a version of 'Birth', to have a rough live version on CD9 of the

Focus 50 Years Anthology recorded in Osaka in July 1974 is very useful. This almost twelve-minute version begins with a flute solo and continues with an extended solo from Jan, bringing it to its enhanced length.

'Hamburger Concerto'

So, we came to the piece that essentially splits the audience (including your author). The first writing sessions for this twenty-minute track were held the year previously, as the band struggled – in vain – to write 'Vesuvius', the follow up to 'Eruption', in Chipping Norton. Completed three years after their first side-long effort, there's very little to link the two pieces, aside from their length. Whereas 'Eruption' contains extreme dynamic and tonal shifts, 'Hamburger Concerto' is built around a very static bass and drum groove which, no matter how good the playing, some listeners have found a little dull. The piece begins well and ends superbly, but the track feels very flabby during its middle ten minutes. This is a criticism often aimed at twenty-minute pieces. Think 'The Remembering' from Yes' *Tales From Topographic Oceans*, for instance. The very best have no filler, and we know that 'Eruption' was created from some judicious editing from Mike Vernon. 'Hamburger Concerto', however, feels flabby. There are some aimless sections here and there, a funereal pace at times and a central guitar solo from Jan that, while brilliantly played, seems overlong, like a few of the guitar and flute solos on *Focus 3*.

Others disagree, of course. Peet Johnson reveres Jan's solo in 'Medium II' as 'a resplendent musical panorama'. He's right, of course; it's a terrific solo, but my argument is that it is too long to serve the overall piece. The judicious editing from three years previously is absent. In the end, the listener should be the judge, and for many, this is Focus' masterwork.

There is some dispute as to who came up with the name in the end. Some say Jan, but Colin Allen also lays claim to it. It's all a conceit, of course – a device to link some disparate pieces of music – and a rather cheesy one at that. According To Peet Johnson, two other tracks were also considered for inclusion. 'P's March' was the only track considered good enough for release from the 1973 Chipping Norton sessions, although having Pierre playing on it must have been considered difficult. 'Focus IV' was also demoed in January 1974 but was not completed. It was to appear on *Mother Focus*, making *Hamburger Concerto* the first Focus album, not to include one of the 'Focus' sequence of tracks.

'Starter' (Joseph Haydn, variation by Johannes Brahms, adapted van Leer)

Cheekily only credited to Thijs in the credits, this piece is actually 'St. Anthoni Chorale', fashioned for orchestra by Brahms from a trumpet serenade by Haydn. Thijs plays it on organ and piano, while Bert accompanies, and Jan's volume-control guitar takes the main theme (sounding quite like a trumpet).

'Rare' (Akkerman)

Rather earlier than suggested on the timings on the 2017 *Hocus Pocus Box Set,* we arrive at Jan's main riff, although hints of the Haydn theme remain as well, before Jan's bass and guitar riff take over, with Thijs accompanying on heavy organ and chirps of synthesiser. This is the first time that the repetitive nature of the piece rears it's head, as the riff is repeated just a touch too often, although Thijs' keyboard textures – using Mellotron and synthesiser – are impressive. So far, so good.

'Medium I' (van Leer)

The piece slows to a typical van Leer vocal excursion – including some yodelling. It's bizarre stuff, even for Focus, and after his initial vocal, the piece continues somewhat aimlessly, via a fine organ solo, albeit played over a snail-like tempo, slowing even further to a flute solo played over exotic percussion. We're in problematic territory, now, in my view.

'Medium II' (Akkerman)

The tempo remains slow as Jan's chorused guitar plays an intriguing riff, soon accompanied by bass and drums. This gives way to a guitar solo, again played with great skill. Beginning at funereal pace, the band – drums, bass and organ – gradually increase the tempo beneath, allowing Jan's playing, finally, to soar. It's a long and well-constructed solo but never quite hits the heights of other pieces in the canon. The solo fades away, accompanied by handclaps, in another rather aimless section.

'Well Done' (Jan Pieterszoon Sweelinck, adapted van Leer, lyrics: Joost van den Vondel)

This section, which has similarities to the Gregorian chants on 'Dayglow' from 'Eruption', is another van Leer adaptation, this time of a Dutch Christmas Carol by playwright Joost van der Vodel with a melody by Jan Pieterszoon Sweelinck. Thijs overdubs vocals with an organ accompaniment. Here it feels tacked on – included for its own sake, rather than to help build the atmosphere of the overall piece, as the corresponding piece in 'Eruption' so ably does.

'One For The Road' (Akkerman)

Again, far longer than the credit on the box set sleeve, this final piece is very impressive. Piano arpeggios and Mellotron chorus accompany, while the lead melodies are taken by Jan's guitar and Thijs' synth. The synth solo towards the end, just before the return of Jan's main riff, is wonderful, and the ending – with Thijs' Mellotron suggesting Yes at their most powerful – is spine-tingling.

Bonus Track
'Early Birth' (Akkerman)

This is a short snapshot of the longer piece from the main album, featuring the main themes and a version of Jan's guitar solo when the track slows. The aspect that sets this version apart is the prominence of Thijs flute, plus a lack of harpsichord and while this doesn't really feel 'finished' as such, it's a lovely snapshot of what the final piece might have sounded like. The piece was recorded at early on Olympic Studios in January 1974, so acts as a demo, in effect. Perhaps the inclusion of this or one of the other tracks started at this time might have allowed the main suite to have been tightened. But this was the 1970s. Side-long pieces were in vogue.

Back On Tour

Despite the difficulties with the recording, the band set sail on the *Hamburger Concerto* tour, starting out in Scandinavia in late March – seemingly little more than moments after the album had been completed. All seemed well until Jan walked off stage at a concert in Berlin on 2 April for a full twenty minutes. The band just jammed until the guitarist returned and they continued with the planned set. Thijs suggests that this was due to issues with The Berlin Philharmonic, who were accompanying the band. At the same time, Colin does not recollect any accompaniment at all, remaining mystified at the enigmatic guitarists' short-lived departure.

All seemed fine – as far as it could be – when the band flew to London on 15 April to record a BBC *In Concert* – available to view on DVD one of the *Focus 50 Years Anthology*. The tour continued in the UK in May, ending with two sold-out shows at The Rainbow Theater in London, one of which was filmed for American host Dick Clark's *In Concert* show. This led to tentative (but unrealised) plans for Focus to tour the USA with Eric Clapton, the idea being to feature the world's two greatest guitarists at the time. Yes – Jan was considered *that* good in 1974. A jaunt to Japan saw 'Love Remembered' and 'My Sweetheart' (to appear, in slightly Americanised form, on *Mother Focus)* added to the *Hamburger-*dominated set. July saw the band in Australia. Reports of the band's live set suggest that a Focus concert was quite a ride, with 50% of the material on stage planned, but the other half improvised or changed from night to night. This is entirely different from the largely planned sets by the other titans of progressive rock of the era, whose concerts included only rare space for improvised solos or jamming. This must have been a wonder to behold as Jan and Thijs' competitive instincts took their playing to new heights.

August saw the band back in the UK for 'festival season', including a gig at the Reading Festival, while September onwards saw the band return to the USA, playing a variety of shows (though not with Clapton), including concerts on a bill with Joe Cocker and the J.Geils Band. At the latter show, in Erie, Pennsylvania, the Dutch support act were so good that Geils' road crew allegedly cut the cables to Focus's sound system. Recorded in November and broadcast on December 7, the band played on Don Kirshner's TV rock showcase, showcasing *Hamburger Concerto* and another new piece, 'No Hang Ups'.

It's clear that while the group were delivering perhaps their best-ever shows on stage, a private and sometimes brooding Jan was struggling with the 'rock star' trappings, his behaviour sometimes at odds with the more 'team like' attitude of the rest of the band. It's not difficult to understand. This was the era of the guitar hero, and the boisterous attitude of some fans – particularly in the USA – must have been difficult for a man who was much more at home in the Friesland countryside. As the band wound down towards Christmas, they played a successful show in Voorburg on 20 December, alongside other Dutch progressive bands of the same era such as Trace, Earth and Fire and Kayak. However, when Focus' notoriously protective management allowed Jan to play a one-off concert with his old band Brainbox, including old pal Pierre, on New Year's Eve, the cracks started to open into fissures.

1975 – More Drummers Than Spinal Tap

1975 was to be an odd – and, in the end, somewhat unsatisfactory – year for this most dysfunctional of bands. While, on the face of it, Bert maintained his loyalty to Focus only, Thijs was all over the place with two completely different solo albums, and Jan began working on demos for his first solo effort. Indeed, as the year was to show, in the end, it was probably Bert's dedication which allowed one more album with Jan on board to be created. By the end of the year, the band was in intensive care. And as for the occupier of the drummer's stool – the year was to descend into farce.

However, the first music out of the blocks that year was another album in the *Introspection* series.

Introspection 2 – Thijs van Leer
Personnel:
Thijs van Leer: flute
Rogier van Otterloo: arrangements and conducting
Letty de Jong: voice
Produced by Ruud Jacobs
Recording engineer: Dick Bakker
Mied by: Joop Niggerbrugge, John Richards and Dick Bakker
Recorded at Dureco Studios, Netherlands
Highest chart places: Netherlands: 1, UK: did not chart, US: did not chart
Current availability: BGO double CD with *Introspection*

If you have a winning formula, why mess with it? Released in the early part of 1975, this second instalment largely follows the same pattern of its hugely-successful predecessor. However, to these ears, it's a touch more successful. The material is a little more varied, and the orchestral arrangements slightly less overblown – and alongside a version of 'Focus III' there are two more van Leer originals to enjoy.

Once again, however, the use of bass guitar and kit drums, as well as Letty De Jong, do date the album a tad.

'Goyescas No. IV (Quejas o la Maja y el Ruisenor)'
(Enrique Granados)
This familiar piece by Spanish composer Granados is beautifully romantic and acts as a lovely album opener, with Thijs largely performing as part of

the ensemble – prominent but not dominating. Only the light kit drums and bass guitar later in the track give the game away, rather. And, as an extra bonus, there's no Letty to date the piece further. Within the context of the *Introspection* formula, it's a lovely start.

'Rondo II' (Rogier van Otterloo)

It's back to cod-Bach with this commercially-orientated piece by Otterloo himself, a follow up to the successful track on the first album. Again, the kit drums and bass guitar demonstrate that this has 'the single' written over it, while flute, oboe and harpsichord vie for attention, and a few 'na na na nas' from Letty towards the end of this lively and spirited piece don't intrude too much.

'Introduction' (Domenico Cimarosa)

We travel into Italy in the 18th Century for this lovely piece from the Classical period by Domenico Cimarosa. Again, Thijs almost seems to be dueting with the oboe. Here the arrangement, while expansive, is subtle – until that is, more kit drums and the unmistakable soprano of Letty de Jong intrude momentarily.

'Siciliano' (JS Bach)

The influence of Bach weighs heavily over the whole album and here we have a charming piece by the man himself, with harpsichord almost as prominent as Thijs, and Letty used rather more tastefully than on other pieces.

'Focus III' (Thijs van Leer)

If ever a Focus piece was made for an orchestral arrangement, then this is it. The bass guitar here is more appropriate, given its prominence in the original, while Thijs' flute carries the main melody. It's delicately done, with the orchestra interjecting only occasionally, and one feels that Focus fans may actually rather enjoy this, particularly as piano, kit drums and acoustic guitar all make an appearance. Here the combination of popular and classical instrumentation works in tandem, rather than the rock instruments feeling tacked on, as they often do so often on these albums. Slightly annoyingly, the piece fades out. Side one is hardly a lengthy side of music and I could have happily enjoyed a couple more minutes of this.

'Larghetto & Allegro' (Georg Fredrich Handel)

Handel was a German composer best known for his time composing in

London in the 18th Century. These are two pieces that are named after the tempos at which they are played: slow (slower than andante but not as slow as largo) and allegro (lively). They are played straight with Thijs leading (of course), but the harpsichord also prominent. The arrangement is also completely straight. There are no affectations, vocals or rock instruments. The results are simple and captivating. If only the rest of the albums were like this!

'Introspection II' (Rogier van Otterloo)

This is another piece by van Otterloo – the title track, of course. Bach seems, again, to be the main inspiration, and all Otterloo's usual arrangement tricks are there, with oboe and bass guitar prominent. It's a pretty tune, and even when Letty comes in with some wordless vocals, she blends in nicely rather than grating as she so often does, sadly.

'Sheep May Safely Graze' (JS Bach)

This is a rather radical take on a very famous tune, rearranged to allow Thijs' flute to dominate, which works very nicely. Indeed, the contrast between the sections with minimal instrumentation and the full orchestra provide an interesting variation on the formula. It's the longest piece on the second side, but it's subtly arranged and doesn't overstay its welcome.

'Mild Wild Rose' (Thijs van Leer)

Dedicated – as the whole of *O My Love* was – to Roselie Peters, this is the first of two originals by Thijs, and it's not hard to hear a decent Focus piece in there. It's romantic but not quite as 'obvious' as some of the other pieces on the album and so demands a little more of the listener, making it both welcome and one of the record's better tracks.

'Bist Du Bei Mir' (Gottfried Heinrich Stolzel / JS Bach)

Originally an aria from his opera *Diomedes*, this piece by German composer Stolzel was later adapted by Bach, in an arrangement similar to the one presented here. It's another 'straight' rendition, with no rock instrumentation or vocals, and all the better for it.

'Carmen Elysium' (Thijs van Leer)

It's hard to imagine that a track on an *Introspection* album might be better than it's original, but this might just be the case here. Based on 'P's March' from the Chipping Norton sessions in 1973 (and later on *Ship*

Of Memories), it's a return to the pop / classical hybrid, but once again, it works nicely, as the orchestra and vocals here are just bit-part players, with Thijs flute carrying the main melody. Again, it fades out frustratingly early and might easily have been extended at the expense of another of the tracks on this side.

The New Beatles?

Back to Focus, and on the face of it, all seemed well at the start of 1975. The band completed their *Hamburger Concerto*-era commitments with a winter tour of Spain, completed in early February. How to proceed with the next album was now the order of the day. The band were now big enough to attract some big names now that Mike Vernon was no longer in the picture, and the legendary George Martin was approached. Martin spent the weekend with the band in Holland and got along well with everyone, despite the usual – probably unfounded – rumours that Jan had been somewhat dismissive of Martin's talents. He would be delighted to produce their album. One suspects that it was not just his work with the Beatles that attracted him to the band, but his sympathetic recording of instrumental music. *Apocalypse* by The Mahavishnu Orchestra, which Martin produced, had been released in 1974 to great critical claim and no little commercial success, while one of his 1975 projects was to become *Blow By Blow* by Jeff Beck. There was one problem, however. He was not available for a year due to other commitments. The band and their management decided not to wait.

Additionally, the Spanish tour was Colin's last with the band. It had become clear that Jan wanted Pierre back in the group and that his patience with Colin's rather more conventional style was wearing thin. Colin reports an incident in the studio where Jan accused him of experimenting with drum machines or rhythm boxes. In fact, all Colin was doing was using a metronome to replicate playing with a click track. Colin, as a result, was fired by the Focus management and – to add insult to injury – was also charged $11,000 for his pains.

Mother Focus

Personnel:
Jan Akkerman: electric guitars, acoustic guitar, talkbox
Thijs van Leer: organ, synthesisers, electric piano, grand piano, flute, vocals
Bert Ruiter: bass, lead vocals on 'I Need A Bathroom'
David Kemper: drums

Colin Allen: drums on 'No Hang Ups'
Unidentified session player (but possibly Victor Feldman): percussion
Produced by Focus
Hubert Terheggen: Executive Producer
Recorded by Eric Presige and Mike Butcher at Morgan Studios, Brussels and Studio 55, Los Angeles, January to May 1975
Highest chart places: Netherlands: 15 , UK: 23, USA: 152
Currently available as part of the *Focus 50 Years Anthology* box set or on Red Bullet CD

Thijs recorded his solo album *O My Love* in April to June 1975 in Los Angeles, around Focus commitments. *Mother Focus* was demoed in early 1975 and then recorded in Hollywood in May, with some sessions recorded in Brussels earlier in January (with Colin Allen) and earlier in May (with David Kemper) before the move to the USA. Focus went on and toured Australia and Japan in late May and early June of that year, with the album itself, finally released in October.

Two other main changes took place in personnel. With Colin Allen out, versatile American session man David Kemper was drafted in, first of all for the initial album sessions in Europe and also to cover the band's live commitments during the period. Secondly, original Focus producer Hubert Terheggen replaced Mike Vernon behind the mixing console. Nonetheless, Akkerman chose to record his guitar parts away from the rest of the band as he had done with *Hamburger Concerto* the year before. His playing is somewhat dominated by the 'talkbox' guitar effect, to become part of his arsenal for a few years, but most utilised; indeed, some would suggest over utilised, here.

I will lay my cards on the table here. I simply love *Mother Focus.* For me, it is the perfect late-night album – both easy listening and full of melody. It does require a different mindset from the listener, and it's possible that I love this since it taps into an entirely different sort of listening approach that, by sheer coincidence, I also share. Each short track presents a melody, develops it but doesn't overstay its welcome. True, there is little room for improvisation and inspired soloing, but that's not really the point. In some ways, it presages much of the similar-sounding solo material from Akkerman and van Leer would release later in the decade. For all it's homogenous, American sheen, it has a genuinely cohesive vibe, partially because the production sandpapers all the rough edges off the music. It's easy listening but in a very good way. I do, however, accept that I may well be in the minority here. Many Focus fans were horrified by this new direction.

There are indeed frustrations. Some pieces – in particular 'No Hang Ups' and 'My Sweetheart' – seem cut very short to suit the overarching 'easy listening' vibe of the album, and with no track over four minutes long, a return to the master tapes might reveal some interesting additional material. Indeed, reviews were mediocre at best, and this is completely understandable considering the symphonic nature of *Hamburger Concerto*, released just eighteen months before. It must have been something of a culture shock! The album reached number 23 in the UK but only got to fifteen in Holland, reaching a disappointing 152 in the USA.

Despite this reviewer's love of the album, one does wonder, not for the last time as the band's fortunes began to dip, 'what were they thinking?' Given that 1975 was the year that progressive rock reached it's zenith, with even the most mainstream of artists building a little prog into their music – let's not forget that 1975 was the year that Queen recorded *A Night At The Opera*, and had a number one hit with 'Bohemian Rhapsody' – the band's choice to follow a different, more Americanised path, seems a little hasty, to put it mildly.

It is also easy to see Thijs and Bert as instigators of this new direction, but looking at what Jan was to produce for his solo career later in the decade, there's a genuine feeling of lineage there, and while Jan felt little enthusiasm for the material, he did agree to play on it. If there is any 'blame' to be apportioned, he – as well as executive producer Hubert Terheggen – must share some of it. Arguably, it may have been an artistic mistake, but it was also a catastrophic commercial one.

The *Focus 50 Years Anthology* box set version of the album includes rough mixes of eight of the album's tracks with the two 'Vanilla' pieces mixed, at that point, into one long track. These versions do throw up the odd moment of instrumental interest and variation, but those hoping that these early mixes might throw new light on what the album might have sounded like had it not been given that American sheen will probably be disappointed. Obviously, I *like* that sheen, but I also accept that many Focus fans don't, and a remix of the album in 'classic Focus' style would certainly be of interest in a 'what might have happened' sort of way.

Finally, what was the reason for the title? Well, it was as American as the style of music inside. Put it this way, try saying 'Mother Focus' fast and see what it sounds like …

'Mother Focus' (Akkerman, van Leer, Ruiter)

This opener is a smoothed-out version of 'Glider', recorded in Chipping Norton in 1973, which appears on *Ship Of Memories*. Both versions have their merits, and in terms of arrangement, there is relatively little to choose between them. Indeed, of all the tracks on this album, 'Mother Focus' is the most like old school Focus, with a strong and varied palette from Jan, including talkbox guitar, some relatively boisterous rhythm guitar, a lovely, strummed acoustic riff (a sonic feature of this album) and even some well-placed electric sitar. Thijs is prominent on piano, organ and yodelling and the rhythm section locks into a funky groove from the word go.

'I Need A Bathroom' (Ruiter)

Constructed over a basic track recorded by Ruiter and David Kemper (although Colin Allen was originally credited), this is a rather silly blues-rock work out that sounds completely out of place on such a sonically sophisticated album. Jan solos throughout like he's still in Brainbox, although his playing is a little low in the mix, and Thijs contributes some tasty electric piano and string synthesizer. Bert's 'song' – poorly sung by him, but he gets away with it – is throwaway stuff, sounding like a guide vocal for something to come later. The lyrics may refer to the gradual disintegration of the band, but they probably don't mean anything at all, except that Bert needs a toilet break. The song breaks down with an extra few seconds of guitar noodling at the end.

'Bennie Helder' (van Leer)

The album settles into its late-night groove with this charming piece. Again, there are traditional Focus touches, but the track is dominated by Thijs' synthesizers and piano, while Jan's lead guitar lines are largely an afterthought, and it is left to Thijs' flute to provide the main variation. The track closes with a funky break, leading into a flute solo, which then – slightly disappointingly – fades out. In the past, this might have been a prelude to some soloing, but here the track is cut off after its main melody lines have been exhausted. Whether this is a good or bad thing is up to the listener, but the fade-out certainly suits the vibe of the album. Who is Bennie Helder? It was a childhood nickname that Thijs invented for himself. Now you know.

'Soft Vanilla' (Ruiter)

With neither Jan nor Thijs providing much by way of material for this album, the door was open for the band's George (to their John and Paul) to fill in the gaps. Bert's contributions were somewhat derided by the somewhat-ungrateful band at the time, to which the obvious answer from him might be 'where's *your* bloody material, then?' Ruiter must take some credit for bailing out the band and also producing some very decent tunes at the same time.

'Soft Vanilla', to these ears, is charming. It is dominated by a beautifully-judged synthesizer line from Thijs, later doubled by flute, and accompanied by his Fender Rhodes and string synth. This is, undeniably, lift music, but it is, without doubt, a very pleasant lift experience indeed. Jan provides support work here, with some choppy, funky rhythms and acoustic strumming.

'Hard Vanilla' (Ruiter)

Short and sweet, this second part of the two 'Vanilla' pieces lifts the tempo and allows Jan some space to solo low in the mix, albeit with the help of his talkbox, a texture which is not for everyone. The same chord sequences are used as the previous track, with Thijs accompanying on electric piano and Bert laying down some expertly-played jazz-funk bass. The piece almost takes off as Jan's soloing becomes more urgent but disappears into a funky coda. David Kemper's drumming is very tasteful indeed.

'Tropic Bird' (Ruiter)

A mini-masterpiece of restraint and dedication to melody, Kemper lays down a bossa nova beat, while Thijs carries the melody on synth, accompanied by electric piano and little flute fanfares. Jan appears entirely absent, but whether you like this track will depend entirely on your tolerance for this sort of 'late night' vibe. Personally, I think it's a really enjoyable if undemanding, way to end a side of music.

'Focus IV' (van Leer)

This fourth part of the Focus 'saga' returns to rather more familiar territory, with Thijs' lovely piano melody to the fore. When Jan's guitar takes up the same melody, it does so in a restrained way, and even when his lead line moves up an octave, he resists all temptation to overdrive his amp as he might have done a few years earlier. Nonetheless, this all works nicely, and when Thijs' flute takes over the melody, it seems 'right'. The track has two 'bridges' – the first neo-classical in nature, and the second featuring some uncharacteristically heavy-handed synth work, before a final piano, organ and lead guitar coda.

'Someone's Crying...What!' (Akkerman)

This is the first of only two solo Akkerman compositions, and for once, the smoothed out edges don't quite suit a tense piece of music that a couple of years before might have featured organ rather than electric piano (and string synth) and far more prominent electric guitar salvos. The flute lines that feature here would certainly have been played on lead guitar on previous albums. Indeed, it's all a bit of a repetitive plod, and as the piece lifts towards the end, the lead guitar feels a little half-hearted.

'All together...Oh That' (Akkerman)

Things do improve on the following piece, which allows Jan to dominate for perhaps the first – and only – time, with a delightfully-picked acoustic guitar riff, with Thijs' piano providing back up. In fact, this piece develops something of a country vibe, as Jan's slide guitar picks up the main theme and solo's around it in an engaging if restrained fashion. Of course, the vibe of the album probably wouldn't have suited anything more than that, notwithstanding his soloing on 'I Need A Bathroom' of course.

'No Hang Ups' (Paul Stoppelman)

Recorded early on in the album sessions, in Europe, with Colin Allen, we, at last, have a piece of what some might call 'true' Focus, even if it is a 'cover version' of sorts. The track was discovered by Jan when played by Dutch guitarist Paul Stoppelman and immediately made its way into the live set on the *Hamburger Concerto* tour. It is the least affected by the arrangement and production restrictions of the rest of the album and has Jan's most upfront and emotive playing alongside some powerful organ work from Thijs, albeit supplemented, just a little too much, by string synthesiser. It also fades out *way* too early – on past albums, it might have been five or six minutes long – but it is delightful while it lasts.

'My Sweetheart' (Akkerman, van Leer, Ruiter)

It's back to the smooth production and that *Mother Focus* vibe for this charming piece, with melody mainly taken by electric sitar with support from Thijs' flute, piano and string synth. It all works delightfully – even the congas played by an unnamed session man are splendid (though quite possibly played by Victor Feldman, given his involvement in *O My Love*).

Bert even gets to take a short, funky solo, which is pleasing considering his enhanced role on the album. Yet, frustratingly, Jan appears about to cut loose just as the track fades. Another solo lost at the altar of an album's overarching vibe. Played live around the time of recording, the song was also considered strong enough to appear on Thijs' solo album *Nice To Have Met You.*

'Father Bach' (Bach, arranged and adapted by van Leer)
This album closer is an adaptation of a section of Bach's *St. Matthews Passion.* It features organ from Thijs and some volume control guitar work from Jan. In truth, it's fine as a closer but throwaway stuff, and I'd rather have had another minute and a half of either of the previous two tracks. There's little doubt that that material was available to do that, as well. It's a shame.

Bonus Track
'Studio 55 Jam' (Akkerman, van Leer, Ruiter, Kemper)
This is a rather aimless full-band jam recorded during the *Mother Focus* sessions in the USA. Kemper and Ruiter are terrific – the former holding the whole thing together with some razor-sharp playing, while the latter lays down an infectious, funky groove. Thijs vamps along on electric piano, while Jan is present but noodles away without much purpose. It all feels like the band are waiting for him to cut loose – but he never does. It is an interesting piece as it shows how American the band's influences were at the time, but it doesn't really amount to much. Mind you, as it shows that Jan and Thijs were in the studio at the same time, it must be a rarity!

Also recorded at the *Mother Focus* **sessions but released on** *Ship Of Memories* **(or later)**
'Crackers' (Akkerman)
Personnel:
Jan Akkerman: guitars
Thijs van Leer: keyboards, flute
Bert Ruiter: bass
David Kemper: drums
Produced by Focus
Recorded by Mike Butcher at Morgan Studios, Brussels, May 1975

This piece, recorded in 1975 with David Kemper on drums, demonstrates the jazzier, funkier tack that Jan's writing was taking by this time. Thijs' flute is particularly good, and Jan's solo is one of his finest 'smooth jazz' efforts. The odd whooshing guitar effect does irritate a little, and at less than three minutes, the piece is just starting to get going as it fades out. It was to be developed more fully by Jan as a solo piece but is also delightful in this band version. Indeed, I find the Focus take on the track, with Thijs' contributions intact, just a touch more interesting than Jan's solo version, which is lovely but one-paced.

A 'vocal' mix was also created, available for the first time on CD on the *Focus 50 Years Anthology* box set. This is a bit of a misnomer, really, as the only vocal is an effects-laden voice saying the word 'Crackers' (probably) once. Its only other release was on the 1976 Polydor compilation album *Medium Rare*.

The track was originally recorded as a single but was never released. Indeed, as we shall see very shortly, even it's potential release was to become a bone of contention with a certain drummer …

'Red Sky At Night' / 'O Avondrood' (Akkerman, van Leer)

Personnel:
Jan Akkerman: guitars
Thijs van Leer: keyboards, flute
Bert Ruiter: bass
David Kemper: drums
Produced by Focus
Recorded by Mike Butcher at Morgan Studios, Brussels, May 1975
'Red Sky At Night' available on *Ship Of Memories*, 'O Avondrood' available on *Focus 50 Years Anthology*

Recorded in 1975, with David Kemper on drums and Bert absent, this was one of the last collaborations between Jan and Thijs to be released for many years. It was recorded as a 'new' piece to play on the late 1975 tours, though supposedly it rarely made an appearance in the set. It's rather lovely – dominated by Jan's lyrical lead guitar, with Thijs accompanying largely on piano. Bass is played on a synthesiser, with some doubling on the bass notes of Thijs' piano. It has the potential to be a Focus classic but misses a more expansive drummer – Kemper's drumming plods, which is unusual for him, and there's barely a fill in the whole piece. Bert's mobile bass is also missing, so the track has a slightly unfinished feel about it. Thijs' flute solo is delightful, but the track does run out of ideas somewhat towards the end, missing a final element and a loss of a minute from the track's length wouldn't have gone amiss. It is definitely a case of 'what might have been'.

A vocal version was also recorded at the time and was finally released on CD on the *Focus 50 Years Anthology* box set, alongside the video version, shown on *Avro Toppop* on Dutch TV and also available on the second DVD in the box set. The song had previously appeared on the Dutch compilation album *Zing In Je Moerstaal*. 'O Avondrood' had lyrics by Jules Deelder. It is largely the same, but with Thijs singing the main melody in unison with Jan's guitar. In the video, only Jan and Thijs are seen, and, as eagle-eyed viewers who have seen the clip have suggested, it's by no means certain that the two are in the same room. Based on what we know of their relationship in 1975, they probably weren't. Jan looks distinctly uncomfortable, as he so often does in such settings.

O My Love – Thijs van Leer

Personnel:
Thijs van Leer: flute, piano, electric piano, synthesiser
Paul Buckmaster: synthesiser, keyboard bass, cello, percussion, electric piano, piano
Roselie van Leer: vocals
Victor Feldman: percussion
Wilton Felder: bass
James Gadson: drums
Eugene Cipriano: English horn, oboe
David Kemper: drums
Louis Shelton: electric guitar
Norman Benno: oboe
Recording engineer: Eric Prestidge
Recorded and mixed April to June 1975 at Davlen Sound Studios, Los Angeles
Produced, arranged and conducted by Paul Buckmaster
Highest chart places: Did not chart
Not available on CD, but can be heard on Youtube

For Thijs' first solo album outside the 'light classical' genre, he recruited Paul Buckmaster, a British-born cellist and arranger. Paul had worked with many massive stars, including David Bowie and Elton John, and had become a friend of Thijs' wife Roselie (nee Peters). Thijs and Roselie decamped to Davlen Sound Studios in Los Angeles for three months (on and off) in the middle of 1975 to work on the album with Buckmaster and a host of crack LA session men, including David Kemper.

The resulting album – slightly cloyingly entitled *O My Love* – is something of a varied affair but certainly worthy of the CD release it has never (at time of writing) received. The tone of the record is certainly informed by the newly-married couple's feelings for each other, with Roselie heavily involved in the writing and performing, as a vocalist. In truth, her vocals are serviceable rather than strong. She has a fragile, girlish voice, and had her parts been given to a better singer, the album might have itself been stronger.

The record is available to listen to in its entirety on Youtube, and it's certainly worth it. Even though many of the instrumental pieces fall into the jazz-funk genre, they are well played and arranged, with subtle string arrangements. However, some of the tracks feel underdeveloped, and for all their studio sheen, they lack any sort of depth. However, it's unlikely that the listener will come away from the experience feeling cheated. It's all pleasant, undemanding stuff, even if it rarely sounds like 'classic' Focus.

'Street Rondo' (T. van Leer, Buckmaster)
The album opens with this rather tasty mixture of cool jazz-funk and... well... Bach! This instrumental piece is based around a lovely flute riff from Thijs, which occasionally explodes into a neoclassical motif. His Fender Rhodes is also prominent, while the rest of the instrumentation is provided by some of the aforementioned LA session men, including Wilton Felder on bass and the legendary Victor Feldman on congas. Think of a *Royal Scam* era Steely Dan backing track, and you are somewhere close.

'Eddy' (T.van Leer, R. van Leer)
'Eddy' is a strong song, somewhat woefully underrepresented by its recorded outings. Here it features Roselie's – frankly – weak vocal, while on *Focus Con Proby,* it is given rather more histrionic treatment by PJ Proby, as discussed later. Just give it to the right singer, already! The song itself – and the arrangement here – are both lovely; its a gentle yet surging ballad with an insistent hook. Instrumentally, the star of the show is Thijs' on piano and Focus drummer David Kemper, plays the kit here.

'Blue Windmill' (Buckmaster, T.van Leer)
This is another strong jazz-funk instrumental, this time built around two intertwining riffs, one from Fender Rhodes piano and the other Yamaha

YC-45 synth, both played by Thijs. One can almost see him bobbing his head with enthusiasm as he plays this. Flute is also included, but as a soloist rather than a vehicle of thematic propulsion. James Gadson's drumming is also very impressive. The piece does run out of ideas rather quickly but is fun nonetheless.

'Fisthearted' (T.van Leer, R. van Leer)
All of a sudden, we have something a little more Focus-like, with a piece that includes a charming flute refrain. We have a lead vocal, this time nicely performed by Thijs himself. Again, it's a decent enough and tuneful piece, with a charming synth and actual-strings-based arrangement. But again, it feels rather slight and underdeveloped.

'The Gleeman Tonite' (R. van Leer)
The artists wife and producer team up in a strange, brief ditty that has no involvement from Thijs, except (presumably) standing in the control room, looking pleased. This is a vignette of a piece – a short vocal refrain accompanied by cello and tambourine. It seems to have no purpose whatsoever, except to close side one of the record, but it's harmless enough.

'O My Love' (T.van Leer, R. van Leer)
A sumptuous, full-on, 1970s arrangement cannot disguise the weakness of Roselie's vocal. Indeed, the song follows the chord pattern of the instrumental arrangement and need not be there at all, as this is one of the better developed and more cohesive pieces, featuring lovely solos from Buckmaster (synth) and Thijs, who delivers an exquisite flute solo.

'Little Brother' (T. van Leer)
A charming and sensitive duet for piano (Thijs) and Buckmaster (cello) sees the album moving into rather more classical waters.

'Peacemaker I' / 'Peacemaker II' ((T. van Leer)
Two short piano solos from Thijs – they sound improvised but may not be – that mix jazz and classical motifs seamlessly. They are lovely and beautifully played but again add to the feeling of insubstantiality that pervades the album.

'Peacemaker III' (T. van Leer)
This is more like it. The chordal structures begun on the first two pieces

are continued with the full band. Indeed the introduction of some subtle electric guitar and two oboes give this piece some welcome variation. The musical interest is maintained by the track's chord structure, which is full-on jazz. This might please some, but it's hard to imagine fans of classic-era Focus warming to it much. Nonetheless, it's a strong track and an album highlight.

'Little Sister' (T.van Leer, R. van Leer)
A short, fragile vocal piece sung by Thijs, with his flute also prominent. It is reminiscent of 'Moving Waves' (the track) but with a rather more expansive, full-band arrangement. It then runs into:

'What You See' (Buckmaster)
This, on the other hand, is very much a solo instrumental piece from Buckmaster, with his own keyboards – mainly synthesiser – prominent, and Thijs nowhere to be seen. It's rather good, but then – frustratingly – suffers a long fade out just as it's starting to get going. This piece – and 'Little Sister' – were played by the Philip Catherine line up of Focus on their UK tour in 1976 and is covered in the 1976 chapter.

Pierre Returns
So, one Focus album and two solo albums from Thijs had been recorded in little more than half a year. Jan was also working up solo material to appear the following year. What on earth would happen next? With touring planned, the first order of business was to record another piece for that tour (although surely they had a whole album in *Mother Focus* to play, didn't they?). This was the aforementioned 'Red Sky At Night', which had Kemper on drums but no Bert. Kemper, feeling (probably correctly) that Jan didn't respect him, quit immediately after the session. However, Pierre had recently left his post-Focus band Trace, so was available for a return. It was a simple decision on the face of it, of course, although relations at the time between Thijs and Pierre could have been better, as Thijs had publicly proclaimed Colin Allen as the 'saviour of Focus', which had not gone down well with Pierre. Furthermore, Bert had been the main instigator of the *Mother Focus* direction and was opposed to Pierre's return. Pierre's arrival meant a return to (in Bert's mind) an older, less interesting style. Both Bert and Thijs must have feared that real factions would appear in the band, which might become split down the middle. They were to be proved right.

After a West German TV spot, in which Pierre fitted in perfectly, the band were due to tour the Far East. This was never a pleasant journey in the 1970s, and it was made worse when, on their arrival in Australia, Cat Stevens, who was on the same plane as the band, was discovered with some 'undesirable substances' rectally inserted. This threatened the clean-living Dutch band with the same 'investigation', which was thankfully averted by some fast-talking. The Australian concerts were largely well-received, although Jan received some criticism for his continued favouring of the talkbox. The tour then moved on to Japan. The setlist was varied around this time, with some nights featuring extended improvisations (and a lot of talkbox), while 'Eruption' was also played in its entirety on some occasions.

Trouble reared its ugly head when the band returned to Europe, with Summer festival appearances in Roskilde in Denmark and Oslo in Norway. In Norway, there seemed to be a standoff between both factions of the band, with Thijs and Bert playing to the setlist, while Pierre and Jan jammed aimlessly. This is hard to imagine, but it seems that whatever the effect of this was, the crowd were not amused. Jan, it seems, was protesting about the setlist routine in a passive-aggressive manner. In an interview earlier in the day, while praising Thijs' gifts as a composer, he had hinted that he might step back from the 'pop scene' sometime in the near future. Sooner rather than later, by the sounds of it.

As the year rolled by and *Mother Focus* was released to mixed reviews and disappointing sales, Polydor also wanted a new single. Jan donated 'Crackers', which had been recorded at the *Mother Focus* sessions, with David Kemper on drums. Pierre wanted to re-record the drum parts, and Thijs and Bert said no. Pierre quit there and then, meaning that manager Yde de Jong had to postpone a planned UK tour – the band's most lucrative territory – until early 1976. A desperate call was made to David Kemper, who accepted the new position and agreed to fly over for rehearsals early in 1976.

The year finished with a band barely holding itself together. Not for the first time.

Live in Japan 1975

Personnel:
Jan Akkerman: guitars, talkbox
Thijs van Leer: keyboards, flute, vocals
Bert Ruiter: bass, vocals

Pierre van der Linden: drums
Recorded at Nippon Budokan, Tokyo, 21 June 1975
Mastered by Wouter Bessels
Available on *Focus 50 Years Anthology* CD9

CD nine of the *Focus 50 Years* box set features live tracks from 1971 to 1975, including four live pieces recorded at Nippon Budokan in Tokyo on June 21 1975. This was the Japanese tour that took place immediately after the recording of *Mother Focus*, but well before it's release, with Pierre back on drums. It is hard to escape the conclusion that – even with the band's level of musicianship still on full display – that all is not well in the band. To me, except 'House Of The King', these tracks are an interesting, if quite a tough, listen. Had you been in the audience at those concerts, would you have expected the full Focus live experience? Perhaps some old classics and some new material? It's interesting that the band decided to fall back on improvisation – a strong part of Focus' approach to music, of course – but often challenging for the listener.

'Improvisation #1' (Akkerman, van Leer, van der Linden, Ruiter)

This first eight and a half minute improvisation has similarities to the 'Studio 55 Jam' in that it is built around a terrific, funky riff from Bert, with Pierre playing a shuffling accompaniment. Both Thijs and Jan take solos, with Thijs contributing fluid Fender Rhodes runs, while Jan's is far more angular with occasional bursts of speed and talkbox. It's actually pretty good, albeit a little aimless, as jams can sometimes be.

'House Of The King' (Akkerman)

This is a super-speedy rendition, with Jan's guitar very flanged in the flute-led sections, and his solo nicely judged (but of course, nothing like the original). There's a (presumably/hopefully) playful pause before the final flute passage. It's a decent version.

'Improvisation #2' (Akkerman, van Leer, van der Linden, Ruiter)

An almost marching beat from Pierre sees Bert improvising on an effect-laden bass (and accompanying grunts) while Jan vamps. It's the arrival of Thijs' organ that gives the piece a structure, while Jan's lead line is also very effective later in the song. This piece works well, as it sounds

Our two protagonists – Jan Akkerman (above) and Thijs van Leer (below) – in typical poses. Both shots were taken during BBC appearances; Jan in May 1972 and Thijs in April 1974. (*BBC / Red Bullet / Wouter Bessels*)

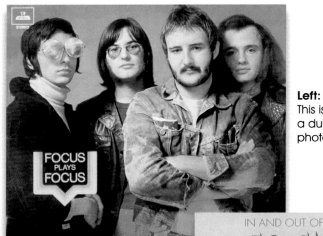

Left: *Focus Play Focus*, 1970. This is the Dutch release, using a dull but effective full band photograph. (*Red Bullet*)

Right: *In And Out Of Focus*, 1970. For English language fans, this will be the more familiar title – and cover – for the debut album. (*Red Bullet*)

Left: *Focus II*, 1971. Again, this is the 'psychedelic' cover for the Dutch edition of the follow-up. (*Red Bullet*)

Right: *Moving Waves*, 1971. English-language purchasers will be far more familiar with the US / UK version of the album. It is – arguably – the band's finest achievement. (*Red Bullet*)

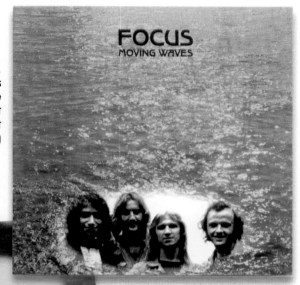

Left: The same cover the world over (at last) for the band's third album *Focus 3* in 1972, although it's hardly a design classic. (*Red Bullet*)

Right: *Hamburger Concerto* in 1974 offered an elegant – if rather grey – cover with a nicely done gatefold. (*Red Bullet*)

Left: Thijs and Jan performing next to each other on the *Old Grey Whistle Test* in May 1972. (*BBC / Red Bullet / Wouter Bessels*)

Right: Perhaps the unsung hero of the 'classic' Focus line up, the fabulous Bert Ruiter, here seen offering a rare vocal during 'Eruption' in May 1972. (*BBC / Red Bullet / Wouter Bessels*)

Left: Pierre van der Linden in 1972, whose unique playing style influenced so much of the band's music from 1971 to 1973. (*BBC / Red Bullet / Wouter Bessels*)

Right: Thijs – mid-yodel – in May 1972. (*BBC / Red Bullet / Wouter Bessels*)

Left: Jan's iconic 'Black Beauty' Les Paul, his main weapon of choice in the band's early years. (*BBC / Red Bullet / Wouter Bessels*)

Right: The full band in complete harmony in May 1972. If only that harmony had lasted! (*BBC / Red Bullet / Wouter Bessels*)

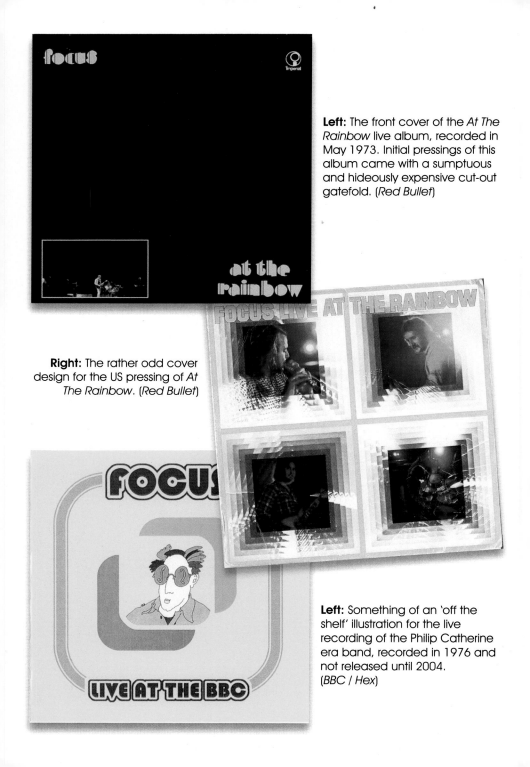

Left: The front cover of the *At The Rainbow* live album, recorded in May 1973. Initial pressings of this album came with a sumptuous and hideously expensive cut-out gatefold. (*Red Bullet*)

Right: The rather odd cover design for the US pressing of *At The Rainbow*. (*Red Bullet*)

Left: Something of an 'off the shelf' illustration for the live recording of the Philip Catherine era band, recorded in 1976 and not released until 2004. (*BBC / Hex*)

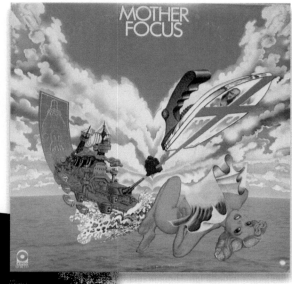

Right: *Mother Focus*, 1975. An odd cover for an album that is much-derided by some Focus fans. (*Red Bullet*)

Left: The *Ship Of Memories* compilation, curated by Mike Vernon and released in 1977. (*Red Bullet*)

Right: The last Focus album of the 1970s, *Focus Con Proby* in 1978. The album combines jazz fusion instrumentals with songs sung in an overwrought manner by Proby. (*EMI / Red Bullet*)

Left: Thijs sports rather more extravagant stage wear for the *Hamburger Concerto* tour in 1974. Note also the larger keyboard rig. (*BBC / Red Bullet / Wouter Bessels*)

Right: Even Jan has smartened up for the BBC in 1974. The stage wear is fashionable, the hair is neat, the beard has gone and the guitar is new! (*BBC / Red Bullet / Wouter Bessels*)

Left: New drummer Colin Allen, recruited in a hurry when Pierre left the band at the end of 1973. Thijs called him the saviour of Focus. Pierre disagreed. (*BBC / Red Bullet / Wouter Bessels*)

Right: Thijs sings 'O Avondrood' on film in 1975. (*Avro-Tros / Red Bullet / Wouter Bessels*)

Left: Jan may or may not be in the same room as Thijs for the 'O Avondrood' promo film. (*Avro-Tros / Red Bullet / Wouter Bessels*)

Right: Jerry Boys (left) and Mike Vernon (right) discuss *Moving Waves* in a 1997 documentary, available (in Dutch) as part of the *Focus 50 Years Anthology* box set. (*KRO-NCRV / Red Bullet / Wouter Bessels*)

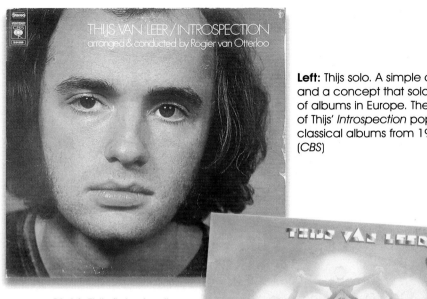

Left: Thijs solo. A simple cover and a concept that sold millions of albums in Europe. The first of Thijs' *Introspection* popular classical albums from 1972. (*CBS*)

Right: Thijs first solo album outside the 'light classical' genre, *O My Love* from 1975. It was recorded in the USA at around the same time as *Mother Focus*. It deserves the re-release that it has never had. (*CBS*)

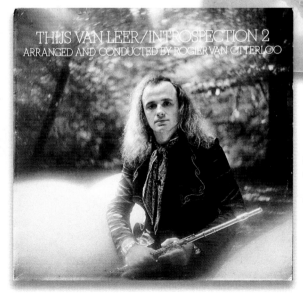

Left: The hair is a little longer, but otherwise, it's another studied cover for *Introspection 2* (1975). It was almost as successful as the first one. (*CBS*)

Right: A minor success but a lovely, restful Christmas album. *Musica per la Notte di Natale* from 1976. (*CBS*)

Left: *Introspection 3*, 1977. A man and a flute, Enough said. It was another big success. (*CBS*)

Right: *Nice To Have Met You*, 1978. This was Thijs' next 'pop' project, forged by the connections he made as part of the CBS Jazz All-stars at the Montreux Jazz Festival in July 1977. Despite a proggy cover, the contents are pure jazz-funk. (*CBS*)

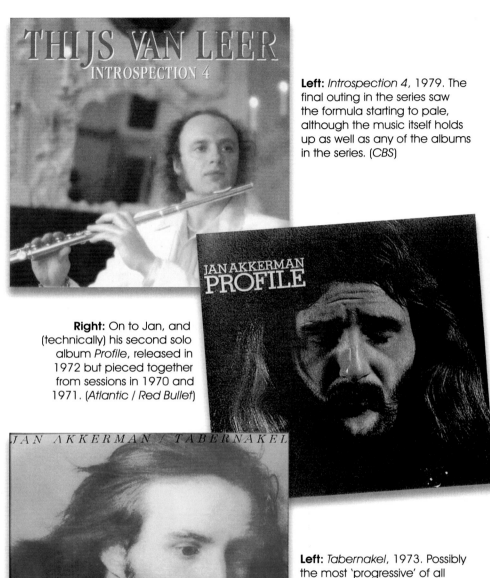

Left: *Introspection 4*, 1979. The final outing in the series saw the formula starting to pale, although the music itself holds up as well as any of the albums in the series. (*CBS*)

Right: On to Jan, and (technically) his second solo album *Profile*, released in 1972 but pieced together from sessions in 1970 and 1971. (*Atlantic / Red Bullet*)

Left: *Tabernakel*, 1973. Possibly the most 'progressive' of all the early Focus solo albums, it combines solo lute pieces with some expansive, neoclassical full-band arrangements. (*Atlantic / Red Bullet*)

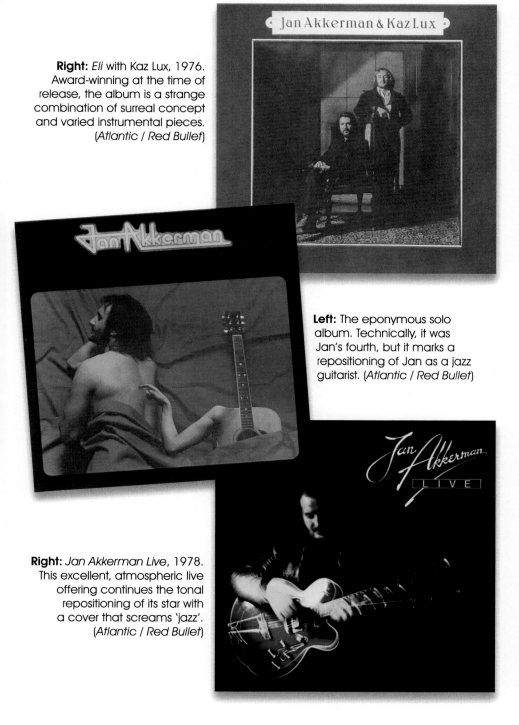

Right: *Eli* with Kaz Lux, 1976. Award-winning at the time of release, the album is a strange combination of surreal concept and varied instrumental pieces. (*Atlantic / Red Bullet*)

Left: The eponymous solo album. Technically, it was Jan's fourth, but it marks a repositioning of Jan as a jazz guitarist. (*Atlantic / Red Bullet*)

Right: *Jan Akkerman Live*, 1978. This excellent, atmospheric live offering continues the tonal repositioning of its star with a cover that screams 'jazz'. (*Atlantic / Red Bullet*)

Left: *Arunjez*, 1978. A diversion into classical music, albeit with a jazz sheen and played on the electric guitar. (*Atlantic / Red Bullet*)

Right: *3*, 1979. Jan's final solo album of the 1970s has a rather more commercial feel with two vocal pieces and a smooth jazz-funk and soul vibe. (*Atlantic / Red Bullet*)

Left: Not a Jan solo album, but a significant guest appearance. *Two Sides Of Peter Banks* was the former Yes man's 1973 debut solo album. It utilised various improvisations recorded with Jan in 1972. Jan was not a fan. (*Sovereign*)

Right: Philip Catherine plays 'Angel Wings' on *The Old Grey Whistle Test* in 1976. A brilliant jazz fusion guitarist, the amiable Belgian had the simple disadvantage of not being Jan Akkerman. (*BBC*)

Left: American session drummer David Kemper with Focus in 1976. During a turbulent fifteen-month period, from the start of 1975 to the spring of 1976, Focus actually had three drummers. (*BBC*)

Right: The 'classic' line up reunited briefly for *Veronica Goud van Oud* in 1990. Jan had also developed some stagecraft and even appeared to be having fun! (*RTL / Red Bullet / Wouter Bessels*)

JAN AKKERMAN & THIJS VAN LEER

FOCUS

Left: *Focus*, 1985. This collaboration between Thijs and Jan was poorly received and has dated very badly due to its very '1980s' arrangements, but it still has some very decent moments. (*Vertigo / Mercury / Red Bullet*)

Right: *Hocus Pocus – The Best Of Focus*. The essential one-disc Focus compilation, even if the tracklisting is questionable. (*Red Bullet*)

THE BEST OF

FOCUS

HOCUS POCUS

9CD+2DVD

focus

50 YEARS

ANTHOLOGY 1970-1976

Left: *Focus 50 Years Anthology 1970-1976*. Released in 2020, this amazing nine CD and two DVD boxed set covers the Akkerman era. It was lovingly compiled and remastered by Focus / Jan Akkerman archivist Wouter Bessels. (*Red Bullet / Wouter Bessels*)

like an end of concert introduction to something else, rather than a piece in its own right, which indeed it does seem to be, as the piece then transitions rather uncomfortably into:

'Hocus Pocus' (van Leer, Akkerman)

Jan vamps around the main chords unconvincingly (it has to be said) while Pierre accompanies, before a burst of yodelling brings us into very brief rendition of the band's best-known song. It may actually be a reprise after an earlier, fuller version – in fact, I hope it is because I'd feel very short-changed if this were it. This version feels messy and slightly unsatisfactory.

1976 – Catherine Wheel

The rigours of touring – playing the same material night after night while staying in soulless hotels in unfamiliar towns – do not suit everyone. While Jan has done his fair share of touring since his days in Focus, his struggle with commitment to the material he was playing, the lack of (in his mind) genuine improvisation in the set and his disinterest in the musicians with whom he was playing, meant that a split was all but inevitable.

It has been alleged – denied by Thijs – that Jan was fired at the end of 1975 or that he merely sat out his contract. What does seem to have happened is that, with a British tour in the offing in the early part of 1976, Jan was dragged to a rehearsal at the band's regular rehearsal facility at the Kasteel – hardly a well-heated space in the first place – while he was suffering from flu. The band began playing the tune that was to become 'Maximum' when Jan started to argue with Thijs and Bert, and then Thijs snapped – essentially firing Jan. It was mid-February 1976. A UK tour – which had already been postponed once – was just days away, and the band had no guitarist.

What could the band do in these circumstances? The best long-term bet might have been to cancel the tour and to take stock. But a huge amount of tickets had been sold and to cancel so close to it might have led to financial disaster. Yet, it is important not to understate the influence that Jan had had on the record-buying public of the early 1970s. To many, he was a hero, ranked alongside and even ahead of such musicians as Jimmy Page and Ritchie Blackmore, if the music press polls were to be believed. While he was hardly a showman, he let his technique do the talking. His sudden loss was a massive blow for fans. Furthermore, news did not travel fast in these pre-internet days. The first time many fans would have known about any change in the line up would have been when they arrived at the venue. To put it mildly, it was not ideal.

For Thijs, Bert and manager Yde de Jong, the only option was to find a new guitarist – and fast. Not only would such a musician need to be available at almost no notice, but he would need to be brave – or naive – enough to take on a potentially hostile audience. But their luck was in. Old friend Ruud Jacobs informed Thijs that Belgian jazz guitarist Philip Catherine was at that very moment rehearsing at Ruud's house in Hilversum with veteran harmonica player Toots Thielemans. Thijs was soon there jamming with the pair, and in a trice, Catherine was recruited.

The amiable Belgian had been around in the jazz scheme for a good fifteen years at this point. As well as several solo albums, he had played with two violin legends in Stephane Grappelli and with Jean Luc Ponty in his (pre-fusion) quintet. By the mid-1970s, Catherine had drifted further into the fusion scene, as had many jazz musicians of the time (including Ponty), inspired by the success of Miles Davis.

The advantages of having Catherine in the band must have been obvious. For a start, he was pleasant to work with, he was available and he was used to working from charts, which would be necessary at the start of the tour, at least. Furthermore, as a jazz musician, there was some synergy with the direction in which Thijs and Bert now wanted to take the band. There would have been a real hope that he would suit the new fusion-orientated material that the band planned, even though he had not heard of Focus, let alone listened to any of the bands material. However, UK audiences would have expected something very different.

Thijs brought the guitarist to Baarn for rehearsals, which were further disrupted by the brief absence of David Kemper, who had flown back to the USA to visit his ill mother. Nonetheless, with Thijs writing the guitar parts out on charts, to be taped to the back of chairs, the four musicians cobbled together a fairly short set. There seems to have been little compromise in the track selection. On the face or it, a safe move might have been to pack the set with 'hits' to keep an audience, reeling from the loss of Jan, at least partially satiated. But no, the majority of the set was comprised of new – and to an audience unfamiliar – material, some of which was provided by Philip Catherine himself.

To be fair, there must have been some optimism that audiences would embrace this new version of Focus and that after the tour the band could consolidate and record a new album. That, sadly, would not take place for another eighteen months and in very different circumstances. However, both new members have fond memories of the music they played on the tour, even if the reaction of some of their audiences wasn't quite what they would have hoped for. Certainly, Jan (and Pierre's) sometimes surly demeanour on tour was replaced by a far more communal and good-natured spirit, as the band worked their way around the UK. At the end of the day, this was probably the wrong band for the band's audience and the venues into which they had been booked. A jazz band that was playing rock venues to rock crowds. It just didn't work.

Live at the BBC (released 2004)
Personnel:
Bert Ruiter: bass
David Kemper: drums
Philip Catherine: guitar
Thijs van Leer: keyboards, flute, yodelling, vocals
Mastered By Russell Pay
Released by Hux recordings, licensed from BBC Worldwide recordings
Highest chart places: did not chart

Up until 2020, there are only two official – or at least semi-official – long-form audio recordings of Focus live in the 1970s. However, their regular television appearances have at least provided a piecemeal archive of their tours. Indeed, the late winter UK tour of 1976 was recorded twice by the BBC, once when a few pieces were recorded by *The Old Grey Whistle Test* on February 24 and then when a much longer live set at London's New Victoria Theatre (now the Apollo Victoria) was recorded for Brian Matthew's *In Concert* show on BBC Radio One. It is this set that was finally released by Hux Records in 2004.

To these ears, while a couple of the arrangements of the newer pieces are certainly overextended, it's hard to fault Philip Catherine's performance. But he's a jazz guitarist, and when the emotional heft that Jan Akkerman would have brought to some of the pieces is needed, it's simply not there. In planning a change of direction and sticking to it despite the loss of (arguably) their best-loved member, Thijs and Bert made a rod for their own backs. They were playing minority music for an audience in the UK that wanted progressive rock. No wonder they struggled. But there's some really good music in their performance, not least of all the two Philip Catherine pieces 'Sneezing Bull' and 'Angel Wings'

'Virtuous Woman' (van Leer)
The band had used this track during the 1975 tours, partially as a vehicle for Jan Akkerman's talkbox work, and so this was very much 'tried and tested' by this point – in theory at least – although it was never to appear on a studio album. It begins well – Focus always loved an atmospheric opening, and here it's based around organ chords and Thijs' typical vocalisations. Catherine's main guitar theme is also spellbinding and very

'Focus'. The piece does, at this point, however, take its time to get going, as it settles into a faintly aimless slow jazz-funk plod, with some excellent work again from the guitarist. The limelight them moves to Thijs, scatting along to a Fender Rhodes solo. A sudden pace increase surprises and contains another fine jazz solo from Catherine before returning to the jazz-funk and a quiet finish, with a brief 'Bennie Helder' quotation from Thijs.

To these ears, this is all brilliantly played but rather unsatisfactorily structured. It feels like a work in progress that needs some kinks ironing out in a recording studio. As it is, as an opening track, it doesn't quite deliver. Perhaps a shortening of the slow funk sections and an increase in that surprise – but short – uptempo section later might have worked better. It is, however, nowhere near as bad as some commentators and reviewers have suggested, and considering how long the band had been together as a unit – just six weeks – it's remarkably tight. David Kemper sounds like a real find, too.

'Blues In D' (Ruiter)

This shorter, more tightly arranged, and actually rather decent, if you like this sort of thing – I do. It is noticeably funkier than anything that Ruiter wrote for *Mother Focus*. Once again, everyone gets their moment in the limelight, with Bert and David Kemper really gelling. Philip Catherine delivers solo with a slight Latin tinge – reminiscent of Al Di Meola. Indeed, the piece is, in reality, just a showcase for a few solos, with Bert's writing presumably chordal rather than melody-based, so perhaps a jazz-based theme to build a longer piece around might have given the piece more 'heft'.

'Maximum' (van Leer, Ruiter)

Read ahead, dear reader, and you will find that I rather like the version of this piece that appears on *Focus Con Proby*. Here, however, it just ambles along amiably enough in jazz-funk style. What on earth must have the Akkerman fans have thought, assailed as they are here with head-bobbing slow funk and Fender Rhodes chirps served up with string synthesiser. Some excellent lead work (as always) by Catherine really impresses, however, and four minutes in, the track threatens to become a much more Focus-like neo-classical piece. But the guitarist isn't quite up to the transition, and with Thijs favouring electric piano over organ, it's another section that lacks impact before returning to the main 'theme' (such as it is) in a rather aimless fashion. There's a bit of an 'is it over yet?' feel about this one, and a transition to something more Focus-like at eight minutes misses the power that Jan might have given it, even in this over-extended form. When Catherine's melodic solo comes at eight minutes – you can almost *feel* him reading Thijs' charts as he plays it – the performance really lacks impact, well played though it is. What might have been a big, emotional finish is rendered toothless by the jazziness of the playing. But it doesn't finish there – we get a reiteration of the main theme and then a quiet ending. It's well enough received by the audience, but the track itself is at least five minutes too long.

'Sneezing Bull' (Catherine)
At this point, we go from the ridiculous to the sublime. There are several versions of this excellent piece to enjoy, should you wish to. Philip Catherine originally performed it for his album *Guitars* in 1975, when it was recorded only with overdubbed guitars and no other instrumentation. There are clips of him playing it on Youtube at that time, using backing tapes. Here this experiment is repeated with – after a brief full-band introduction – the guitarist using tapes to add extra guitars as he plays an acoustic. The masterstroke – and the thing that makes this piece so appropriate for Focus – is that the superb melody line is doubled on the flute. It could specifically have been written for Thijs to play, and unlike the earlier pieces in the set, it feels … right. The *Focus Con Proby* version is a full-band fusion workout, of course, and probably represents the 'definitive' version (by Focus at least), but after the tedium of 'Maximum', this must have been a real stiffener in a live setting

'Sonata For Flute' (JS bach, adapted van Leer)
This is an adaptation of Bach's *Sonata For Flute or Recorder and Harpsichord in E Flat Major*. It's played unaccompanied by Thijs, in a wonderful performance. But is this set filler? You decide.

'House Of The King' (Akkerman)
Ah, familiarity at last, with this non-essential version of a timeless classic. Catherine's solo begins uncomfortably, but this is actually quite a decent, jazzy version of Jan's original take on the track. Again, however, emotional heft is decidedly absent, but it's a lively variation on the piece, nonetheless, with Thijs giving it everything he's got.

'Angel Wings' (Catherine)

Now we come to another Philip Catherine piece – originally recorded in 1975 for a full-band project called Passport. We're in classic fusion territory, here, strongly influenced by Return To Forever to these ears, in a piece that already has a viable and powerful live arrangement which Focus reproduce with skill. It's a showcase for some astonishing soloing from the guitarist, once again channelling Al Di Meola for all he's worth. The band support superbly, although David Kemper is also a major star here – his drumming is astonishing. While Philip Catherine's playing may not have had the emotional impact of Jan Akkerman's, in the right circumstances, he really could let loose, and this piece genuinely feels too short. It's a real shame it didn't make it onto *Focus Con Proby*. Its presence as part of the shorter *Old Grey Whistle Test* set shows that the track was well favoured at the time, and rightly so. It's splendid.

'Little Sister' (van Leer, Roselie Peters)/ 'What You See' (Paul Buckmaster)

With the band fishing around for suitable material and making a very obvious effort to play as few existing pieces as possible, it's perhaps inevitable that two van Leer solo tracks should make it into the set. Here, we have the two tracks that close Thijs' 1975 solo album *O My Love*. I rather like Thijs' tender – if somewhat pitchy and uncomfortable – rendition of the song itself, which then powers up into a full-band interpretation of the closing piece from that album, written by Paul Buckmaster. Originally based around a jazzy Fender Rhodes-orientated arrangement, this version really benefits from Philip Catherine's playing, not to mention another terrific performance from David Kemper. It is possible that many listeners may cringe a tad at Thijs part scat/ part yodelled accompaniment, presumably there for some end of set excitement. The piece ends on a reprise of 'Little Sister' and fades away...

'Hocus Pocus' (Akkerman / van Leer)

Much of the dislike of this set hinges on the version of 'Hocus Pocus' played by the band on the tour. There's no doubt that while previous live versions that showcased both Thijs and Jan, here it's Thijs show, with Philip Catherine simply playing the chords of the main riff, without offering up a single solo (except in the rock n roll ending) while David Kemper gets two short solos. This is hardly surprising – how could Catherine compete? It's still a shame, though. He does get a rousing round of applause when his name is called in the band introductions – bigger than Bert or David – so he must have made some sort of impression, but to play the track this way is a mistake and perhaps illustrates why so little existing Focus material was played in the set.

Eli – Jan Akkerman and Kaz Lux

Personnel:
Kaz Lux: vocals
Jan Akkerman: guitars, bass, arrangements
Jasper van't Hof: keyboards
Rick van der Linden: keyboards
Warwick Reading: bass
Pierre van der Linden: drums
Richard DeBois: drums
Neppie Noya: percussion
Maggie MacNeil: backing vocals
Margriet Eshuis: backing vocals
Patricia Paay: backing vocals
Produced by Richard DeBois and Jan Akkerman
Recording engineer: Jan Schuurman
Recorded at Soundpush Studios, Blaricum, Netherlands
Released October 1976
Highest chart placing: Netherlands: 4, UK: did not chart, USA; did not chart
Current edition: remastered CD as part of *Complete Jan Akkerman* box set and as a BGO double CD with *Tabernakel*

What next for Jan? Wouter Bessels' sleeve notes for Akkerman's self-titled debut released in 1977 tell us that the demos for that album were worked up in 1975 while he was still in Focus. After his departure, the material for the solo album and this high-concept duo album with his friend Kaz Lux, was recorded – using largely the same group of musicians and crew – at Soundpush Studios in Blaricum. While the basic tracks for the solo album were shelved pending further recording, as we shall see shortly, the resulting duo album, *Eli,* was completed and released in the autumn of 1976.

Kazimierz Lux had played with Jan in Brainbox, leaving after Jan in 1971. He had then embarked on a solo career, which included a 1973 album *I'm The Worst Partner I Know* that had been produced by Mike Vernon at his Chipping Norton studio, with contributions by Jan. *Eli,* however, was to be a concept album based around the surreal journey of the titular woodcutter. Think a folksier *Lamb Lies Down On Broadway*. As the project developed, however, with Jan and Richard DeBois producing, three instrumental tracks were added – essentially Jan Akkerman solo pieces.

The album was a commercial success in Holland, winning an Edison Award as 'Best Album'. It has to be said, however, that it has non worn particular well. The problem is that Lux's vocal delivery – a mixture of singing, spoken word and soul-style scatting – is an acquired taste, to put it mildly. It was probably a tough listen for some at the time, and it remains so now. Even his singing style – very much in the blues/soul genre – jars occasionally. Additionally, the story itself is somewhat impenetrable and is dotted across the album in a fairly non-linear fashion. Musically, of course, it's a different story, with Jan reigning in his virtuosity to deliver a subtle and sympathetic backing to Lux's concept. Significantly, keyboard player Jasper van't Hof was to wind up in Jan's backing band for the next couple of years, while Pierre van der Linden also contributed some of the drums.

In the end, *Eli* feels like an album of two parts, almost as if Kaz Lux either ran out of material or didn't have the confidence to make the whole album in the jazz-funk and vocal style he set out to do. There is little doubt that in anyone else's hands but Jan's, this might have been a disaster, but Jan's vision saves it, even if the instrumental pieces do feel a little tacked on. Whether any listener today will want to play much beyond the three instrumentals is another matter, but it's still worth a listen.

'Eli' (Akkerman / Lux)
Beginning with a lengthy acapella section sung by Lux, he is joined by Akkeman and then the whole band laying down a slow funk accompaniment as Lux introduces his story. It's probably the most accessible vocal track on the album.

'Guardian Angel' (Akkerman / Lux)
We now get into the meat of Lux's story, with Jan's arrangement laying down another funk groove, not dissimilar to a slower version of 'Crackers'. One almost wishes Kaz would shut up for a minute as the playing itself is rather splendid with Warwick Reading's bass work and little percussion interjections from Neppie Noya particularly effective, while Jan plays an effect-laden but highly effective rhythm part.

'Tranquillizer' (Akkerman)
This instrumental piece is a Jan solo track, with the guitarist picking out a steady chord pattern over what sounds like a rhythm box. Sharp-eared listeners will notice a similarity in the chord pattern to 'My Sweetheart' from *Mother Focus,* for which Akkerman had a writing credit along with Thijs and Bert. It's a simple piece yet highly effective.

'Can't Fake A Good Time' (Lux)
We're back into up-tempo jazz/funk territory here, with a continuation of the story and a terrific groove from the whole band. Jan takes something of a backseat, aside from some great rhythm playing, allowing some fantastic keyboard work to take centre stage, including some rather unexpected Mellotron, synth and piano. Again, it's a terrific, powerful groove and despite his sole writing credit, Kaz Lux's vocals feel like an afterthought.

'There He Still Goes' (Akkerman / Lux)
This is another blissful soulful workout and one of the better vocal efforts, as there's even a hint of a 'song' here, bolstered by some soulful female backing vocals. Again, Jan is high in the mix with some great rhythm guitar work and there's also some excellent organ playing here.

'Strindberg' (Akkerman / Rick van der Linden / Lux)
We depart from the story completely here, with this tribute to Swedish polymath August Stringberg. It's a complete departure musically, as well, with Lux singing (and occasionally talking) about the great man with subtle accompaniment from Rick van der Linden on piano and Jan's guitar. It's quite touching, although Lux rather over-emotes when a simpler vocal line might have been more effective.

'Wings Of Strings' (Akkerman)
It's back to Jan solo, with this time a solo twelve-string guitar piece – or perhaps it's two six strings – accompanied by some subtle keyboards, mainly piano and strings. It's beautifully played and recorded and, while it has the aura of an interlude rather than a main piece in its own right, it's beautiful.

'Naked Actress' (Akkerman / Lux)
And so we come to the climax of Kaz Lux's story. This track is largely delivered as spoken word over a rhythm box and rhythm guitar, with brief

interjections of female vocals. Halfway in, Jan introduces an excellent riff as Lux's vocals – largely variations on the word 'perfection' – gather a little urgency with spoken word giving way to impassioned vocalising. It's fairly effective on its own terms but feels like it should go somewhere else with perhaps an up-tempo section. But the piece just … ends.

'Fairytale' (Jasper van't Hof)

Instead, the album closes on a more lyrical note, with this largely synthesised instrumental written and played by keyboard player Jasper van't Hof with some subtle lead acoustic interjections from Jan. Again, it's beautiful, but seems out of place and an odd way to close the album.

Focus Winding Down

Shortly after the band had completed their UK tour, David Kemper returned to live and session work in Los Angeles. The band has a concert booked in Voorburg, so a replacement was needed. In came Maastricht-based American Richard James, who had recorded two albums with a funk band called American Gypsy. He formed a strong bond with Thijs, and the band continued to play across Holland and Belgium. But the gigs – and the attendances – were getting smaller. Thijs began to make more solo appearances playing *Introspection* material and recorded a Christmas album, which we shall look at in a moment. Meanwhile, in July, Philip Catherine even played a Norwegian jazz festival with Jan Akkerman. The pair shared a private plane to and from the event, got along well and even played an improvised duet on Norwegian TV. How ironic.

Things seemed brighter for a while as the band signed a deal with EMI-Bovema, who now had the rights to the band's back catalogue. A new album and a single were promised by the spring of 1977. However, by the end of the year, it seemed that Thijs had put Focus on hold.

But there was unreleased material out there and Mike Vernon and Hubert Terheggen had other ideas, as we shall see shortly.

Musica per la Notte di Natale – Thijs van Leer (with Rogier van Otterloo and Louis van Dijk)

Personnel:
Thijs van Leer: flute
Louis van Dijk: piano, clavinet, arrangements
Frank van Koten: oboe
Joep Terwey: bassoon

Rogier van Otterloo: conductor, arrangements
Concept and production by John J. Vis, Ruud Jacobs
Gijsbert Beths: concertmaster
Albert Kos, Jaap de Jong: sound engineer
Albert Kos, Joop Niggebrugge: mixing
Released on CBS records in December 1976
Highest chart positions: Netherlands: 10, UK: did not chart, US: did not chart
Not currently available on CD, but can be heard on Youtube

Given how successful the first two *Introspection* albums had been in the
Netherlands – and that's *very* successful – it's hardly surprising that the
van Leer / Otterloo team should want to keep the formula going. They did
so with this rather delightful instrumental Christmas album, conceived
by the *Introspection* production team of Ruud Jacobs and John J. Vis. To
the team, the duo added pianist Louis van Dijk. This versatile musician –
who died in 2020 – was best known in the Netherlands for his amazing
versatility, composing, arranging and performing across the classical and
jazz idioms.

As usual, Thijs features on flute, but the arrangements – from both
Otterloo and van Dijk – do not strictly follow the *Introspection* formula.
Instead, they aim at a restful, spiritual and 'Christmassy' vibe. As a
pleasant, albeit niche, collection of traditional tunes, it works very well.
Even the album cover – just embossed text, with the three principles
pictured on the back – serves the relative simplicity of these pieces.
Charting at Christmas in the Netherlands, the album was only a modest
success, reaching number ten in the Dutch charts and hanging around for
only three weeks. The track titles are given in German, English and Dutch,
depending on the provenance of the pieces themselves, while the title of
the album is named in Italian.

In truth, it's very difficult to describe the pieces track by track. The
arrangements are beautiful, very much in a stately, Baroque style,
while the oboe of Frank van Koten and the bassoon of Joep Terwey are
almost as prominent as Thijs' flute on some pieces. Solo piano is also
used frequently, and the string arrangements are almost always subtle
and understated. The familiarity that the listener has with the pieces
will depend largely on what country he or she comes from. Of course,
British listeners will be most familiar with the four pieces that have their
titles in English. On the other hand, there is plenty of cross-pollination

between the German and Dutch-originated pieces, which are well known in both those countries. However, to a British or American listener, the album may not seem sufficiently 'Christmassy' due to the lack of familiar Yuletide tunes. So, what I have attempted to do is to give some idea of the provenance of each piece, including the words for them when sung, even though this is, in itself, an instrumental album. I have also given an English translation of the Dutch and German titles.

Throughout, there is plenty of playfulness on display. It's not until the second verse of 'Hark The Herald Angels Sing' that the most famous melody becomes apparent, and most of the pieces develop and vary their arrangements quite skillfully without resorting to mere repetition. It's a lovely, restful album, and to these ears, it has worn considerably better than the *Introspection* series.

'O Jesulein Süss (O Baby Jesus)' (Johanne Sebastian Bach)
Given Thijs' love of the composer, it's no surprise that the album should kick off with a piece by the maestro himself.

'Coventry Carol' (Traditional)
This is an English Christmas carol dating from the 16th century. The piece was traditionally performed in Coventry in England as part of a mystery play called *The Pageant of the Shearmen and Tailors*.

'Hark, The Herald Angels Sing' (Felix Mendelssohn)
This Christmas carol, hugely popular in Britain, first appeared in 1739 in the collection *Hymns and Sacred Poems*. Although this is, of course, an instrumental version, the carol itself featured lyrical contributions from Charles Wesley and George Whitefield, two of the founding ministers of Methodism, with music adapted from *Vaterland, In Deinen Gauen* by Felix Mendelssohn from Germany.

'Es Ist Ein Ros' Entsprungen' (Literally: A Rose Has Sprung Up)' (Traditional)
This is a Christmas carol of German origin. It is most sometimes translated in English as 'Lo, how a rose e'er blooming' and is sometimes known as 'A Spotless Rose' or 'Behold a Rose of Judah'. The rose in the text is a symbolic reference to the Virgin Mary, and the carol makes reference to the Old Testament prophecies of Isaiah, which, in Christian interpretation, foretell the Incarnation of Christ, and to the Tree of Jesse, a traditional

symbol of the lineage of Jesus. Because of its prophetic theme, the song is popular during Advent.

'Maria Die Zoude Naar Bethlehem Gaan (Mary Would Go To Bethlehem)' (Traditional)

A Dutch carol, beloved of schoolchildren, this tradition piece was first collected by J. Alberdingk Thijm in the book Old and Newer Christmas Songs (1852).

'Vom Himmel Hoch, Da Komm' Ich Her (From Heaven Above To Earth I Come)' (probably Martin Luther)

This is a hymn relating to the Nativity of Jesus, written by pioneering German Protestant Martin Luther in 1534. The hymn is most often sung to a melody, 'Zahn No. 346', that first appeared in 1539 and that was likely composed by Luther as well. That version became a classic Christmas carol, and many composers referred to it in their compositions.

'Er Is Een Kindeke Geboren Op Aard (A Child Is Born From Nature)' (Traditional)

Another popular Duch carol, First published by Lootens en Feys in *Chants Populaires Flamands*, 1879.

'Away In A Manger' (William J. Kirkpatrick)

It's back to the English speaking world for this one. Originally supposed to have been written by Martin Luther, the carol now seems to be of American origin, having first been published in 1882. The musical setting used here comes from Pennsylvanian William James Kirkpatrick, who wrote it in 1895.

'Ich Steh' An Deiner Krippen Hier (I Stand Here By Your Manger)' (Bach)

This is a German Christmas hymn with lyrics by Paul Gerhardt , which were first published in 1653. It was then sung with an older tune by Martin Luther, but this melody was created by Johann Sebastian Bach for Georg Christian Schemelli's *Musicalisches Gesang-Buch* in 1736.

'Hoe Leit Dit Kindeke (How Lies This Little Child)' (Traditional)

It's back to Holland for another traditional Dutch piece.

'God Rest Ye Merry, Gentlemen' (Traditional)

'God Rest You Merry, Gentlemen' is an English traditional Christmas carol. It is in the Roxburghe Collection and is listed as no. 394 in the *Roud Folk Song Index*. It is one of the oldest existing carols, dating to the 16th century or earlier, although the earliest known printed edition is in a broadsheet dated to around 1760. The traditional English melody is in the minor mode; the earliest printed edition of the theme itself appears to be in the 1829 Facetiae of William Hone. The tune has been associated with the carol since at least the mid-18th century when it was recorded by James Nares under the title 'The Old Christmas Carol'.

1977 – Solo Success

Ship Of Memories (1977)
Personnel and credits:
See individual track entries
Released on EMI / Sire records in 1977
Highest chart places: Netherlands: did not chart, UK: did not chart, US: 163
Svailable on *Focus 50 Years Anthology* and Red Bullet CD.

Mother Focus had not been a success, and it's understandable that Hubert Terheggen should still want some sort of return on his investment. So, with that in mind, he asked Mike Vernon to go back through an hour's worth of unreleased material to produce an album of outtakes. Of the nine tracks on the vinyl version of *Ship Of Memories,* six are drawn from the abortive two weeks of sessions at Chipping Norton during 1973 (see that chapter for more detail). Three other tracks come from various other sessions, including an early version of the Akkerman tune 'Crackers' – later to appear on his self titled solo album in 1977 – plus various other recordings. One such – 'Red Sky At Night' – is from 1975 and was discussed earlier.

And the result? Vernon's efforts to remix all this material actually pay dividends, as these tracks genuinely do hang together as an album of sorts. The material itself is also pretty good if lacking the really memorable moments to be found on the other early 1970s albums.

We've dealt with the individual tracks from the compilation as they crop up in the correct chronological sequence earlier in this book.

The Catherine Wheel Stops Spinning
Philip Catherine left Focus a year after he joined, at the start of 1977. There was no acrimonious split; he simply returned to his first love – jazz. It was clear by this point that the band would be unlikely to take on lengthy tours at least for a while, so to remain in the band when he had an alternative career already set up and waiting for him seemed pointless – and completely understandable. He would return later in the year to take part in the final Focus project of the 1970s. But his touring career with Focus was over.

Thijs and Bert now needed further musicians to be 'on call' whenever the band had gigs, and the choice for Focus guitarist was not especially difficult, with Thijs calling on his old friend, the talented Eef Albers.

There's a distinctly laid back vibe to Focus personnel around this time. At a Summer gig in Amersfoort, with Bert unavailable, bassist Wim Essed stood in and with Richard James not having turned up (for unknown reasons) and two sets planned, drummer Henk Zomer, who was in the audience, sat in for the first set while Pierre van der Linden was recruited at very short notice for the second. Given the lack of rehearsal with the two drummers it might have been interesting to see what sort of fist they made of the material. No doubt the high quality of musicianship will have seen them through, but there must have been some hairy moments. For the record, these are the sets on that day, as reported by Peet Johnson:

First set: 'Virtuous Woman', 'How Long' (played as an instrumental), 'Maximum', 'Sylvia' and 'Orion'.
Second set: 'Angel Wings', 'Blues Improvisation' (no surprise there), 'Brother' (sung by Thijs), 'House Of The King' and 'Hocus Pocus'.

Throughout the year, Focus played sporadically while the band mainly occupied themselves with projects outside the group. Richard played freelance gigs, Bert wrote with Dutch band The Knack and Eeef continued with his session work.

Jan Akkerman – Jan Akkerman

Personnel:
Jan Akkerman: guitars, arrangements
Joachim Kuhn: keyboards
Cees van der Laarse: bass
Bruno Castelucci: drums
Pierre van der Linden: drums on 'Floatin''
Neppie Noya: percussion
Strings and flutes arranged by Michael Gibbs
Produced by Richard DuBois
Recorded at Soundpush Studios, Blaricum, Netherlands
Recording engineer: Jan Schuurman
Mixed by Richard DeBois, Jan Schuurman and Jay Denson
Released in September 1977 on Atlantic Records
Highest chart places: Netherlands: 9, UK: Did not chart, USA: Did not chart
Current edition: Esoteric Records, or remastered as part of the *Complete Jan Akkerman* box set

Self-titled albums – especially those released mid-career – often represent a new beginning, and this is certainly the case here. *Eli* is an interesting album, but Jan made it clear that he didn't want to record another like it. His next work would once again show off his instrumental prowess only and would present a more unified vision. Jazz fusion – with a touch of funk – was to be his genre of choice. This is hardly surprising, given Jan's technical ability, not to mention the genres commercial success in the 1970s, with groups like Return To Forever and The Mahavishnu Orchestra having chart entries with albums that, in any other era, would be considered 'niche'.

Pierre played on only one track – 'Floatin'' – with the drum stool otherwise occupied by Bruno Castellucci. Bass was played by Cees van der Laars and – most crucially – keyboards were provided by jazz pianist Joachim Kuhn, rather than the musicians that had played on *Eli*. Kuhn and Akkerman's association would last several years in one form or another. Infact, the previous year – in 1976 – Kuhn had recorded an album *Springfever* which had featured Philip Catherine. The jazz world was, inevitably, a small one.

We have excellent, detailed notes about the genesis of this album thanks to the sleeve notes from Focus archivist Wouter Bessels that accompany the Esoteric reissue in 2016. The tracks were demoed in 1975 and then recording began at the same time as *Eli* during the summer of 1976. The main band then returned to the studio in the late Spring of 1977 to complete the recording, a process that took three weeks. When these basic tracks had been recorded, producer Richard DeBois decided to add strings and flutes to all the tracks except 'Crackers'. British jazz arranger Michael Gibbs, who Jan was aware of as he had recently done some string arranging for US drummer and vocalist Narada Michael Walden, was assigned to arrange and conduct these sessions at Morgan Studios in London.

Some six months before the release of the album, Jan returned to the UK for a lengthy tour with Kuhn in the band. It was his first time in the UK since 1974, and the performance featured a set with Kaz Lux based around *Eli,* which was treated with bemusement by some aspects of the audience. There is also a suggestion that some concerts may have been cancelled due to poor ticket sales.

Had the new album been released by this point, it's quite possible that the tour would have been more successful since the resulting album is supremely well done and there's no doubting the technical abilities of

Jan's brilliant band. A strong album with excellent material, it's certainly Jan's best solo 'band' album of the decade. If there's a fault, it's that the material never really catches fire, and its overall 'smooth jazz' vibe can, at times, be a touch soporific. There are plenty of solos, with Kuhn and Jan both playing with huge skill, but their contributions are somewhat buried by a production that is striving for a homogenous vibe and doesn't really have the confidence to let its stars – particularly guitarist and pianist – come to the fore.

'Crackers' (Akkerman)

Originally recorded by Focus and appearing on *Ship Of Memories*, this funky rendition gets the album off to a lively start. It's a relatively slight tune, though, based around a simple but catchy motif. For most of the piece, it's Kuhn's piano and electric piano that really stand out, with Jan playing a short but sweet solo mid-piece which seems to nod towards Eric Clapton's 'Layla' at one point. This is fair enough; Jan was a huge admirer of the English guitar legend. I will admit to preferring the Focus 'take' of this particular piece on balance, but its development here is still entertaining. Jan based his demo around Focus drummer David Kemper's tight groove on the original, although the American is uncredited.

'Angel Watch' (Akkerman)

Ah – now we have strings. This may have seemed a decent choice at the time, but here they grate a little – they date the album somewhat. That said, they do give the initial part of this piece a little melodic structure and this long track is harmonically complex at the outset, with Jan soloing with some skill and Castellucci's drumming particularly impressive. Three minutes in, we settle into a groove with van de Laars' slap bass dominating, while Jan almost seems to disappear for a while, returning with some smooth lead, followed by a powerful extended piano solo from Kuhn and another extended solo from Jan. This is all very well done, and very worthy, but as a studio piece, it does outstay it's welcome just a tad at just over ten minutes with very little to grab the listener beyond some well-taken jazz solos.

'Pavane' (Akkerman)

This is rather more interesting – a slow-burner of a piece. The track has a serene, almost surreal quality, based around Jan's effect-laden rhythm guitar and an insistent riff. Restraint is the keyword here, and for a while, the listener expects the track to move up a gear, but it doesn't and when Jan solos, the tone of his guitar has an unusual quality, heavy on the reverb. The orchestral strings are also used with restraint and add to the atmosphere. Overall, It's a lovely piece built on the tension between the band and the strings.

'Streetwalker' (Akkerman)
As one might expect from the title of this piece, there's an obvious intention to evoke the rhythm of walking, perhaps late at night on the streets of New York with some nefarious purpose in mind. Again, the strings help add an atmosphere that is very much 'of its time', with the strings even supplying their own melodic line over Jan's mid-song solo. Then, all of a sudden, we're in an Isaac Hayes or Quincy Jones production, and the track smooths out, with Jan providing the occasional tasteful run and a skilful synth solo from Kuhn. Again, this is expertly played stuff, but perhaps a little overlong, the soloists riffing on the same groove for perhaps a few bars too many. But it's hard to deny the skill, and it's a fun listen if a touch on the smooth side.

'Skydancer' (Akkerman)
This is probably the stand out track on the album, and as we would see on *Live,* a real winner in concert. There's real tension here, and Jan's guitar motif is really quite unusual, while the strings provide an interesting counterpoint. There's more than a hint of the classics, here, too, and we realise that this would have made an exciting Focus piece. It might have been interesting to hear what Thijs would have made of it. A funkier section is short-lived, giving way to the main themes once again. There's an interesting little guitar duet on each side of the stereo. All in all, this is very distinctive stuff – one of the few tracks on the album that you feel only Jan could have created.

'Floatin'' (Akkerman)
We return to smooth jazz-funk workouts with this next piece, which again, while beautifully played, particularly by the terrific rhythm section, including the only appearance of Pierre on the album, in full jazz fusion mode. His cymbal work, in particular, is exemplary. It doesn't offer us anything new, particularly, but it's still a good listen. Kuhn tinkles away with a very skilled – and very long – Fender Rhodes solo, but it's too reverb-laden to thrill as it should, and it feels like the keyboard equivalent

of shredding; all speed, but lacking a little soul. Furthermore, Jan feels like a bit-part player for the majority of the piece.

'Gate To Europe' (Akkerman)

The album ends on something a little more tender and heartfelt, with this charming acoustic guitar piece accompanied by shimmering – and probably unnecessary – strings. It's lovely, but the string's feel a little misjudged.

Additional Tracks:
'Angel Watch' (single edit)

This piece was probably chosen as a single for its seemingly commercial funkiness, but it was never going to be a hit, even shorn of its 'difficult' early section.

Montreux Summit Vol One and Two by the CBS Jazz All-stars – Thijs van Leer

Personnel:

Producer: Jay Chattaway

Recording and mixing: Joe Jorgensen, David Richards, Doug Epstein

Mastering engineer: Stew Romain

Executive producer: Bob James

Recorded July 24, 1977, at the Montreux Jazz Festival

Volume One was released in 1977, Volume Two in 1978 on CBS

Current editions. Unavailable on CD and vinyl, but available on streaming services

The Montreux Jazz Festival looms large in the careers of many rock musicians. As well as Jan and Thijs – who have both been extensively involved in the event over the years – bands like Yes and Toto have recorded live shows there. The 11th festival in 1977 was a very special event in that it featured performances on 24 July 1977 by an astonishing host of CBS-signed jazz legends, playing in a variety of combinations. The line up across the two albums reads like a who's who of mid- 20th-century jazz legends:

Bob James, George Duke, Billy Cobham, Ralph MacDonald, Steve Khan, Janne Schaffer, Eric Gale, Stan Getz, Woody Shaw, Alphonso Johnson, Dexter Gordon, Benny Golson, Bobbi Humphrey, Maynard Ferguson, Hubert Laws, Billy Brooks, Peter Erskine, Slide Hampton, Bob Militello and Thijs.

Thijs played as full a part as anyone, playing synthesiser and – mainly – flute. He appears on five tracks across the two albums, and while we will only look in any sort of detail at the tracks on which he plays, it's also interesting to note that a piece on which he doesn't play – Alphonso Johnson's 'Bahama Mama' – was to appear, in diminished form, in *Nice To Have Met You.* Indeed, it was the connections that Thijs made at this prestigious event – particularly with virtuoso percussionist Ralph MacDonald – that led to the recording on that album the following year. Two double albums were released from the show, featuring long pieces and many solo sections, meaning that Thijs' contributions are sometimes obscured, especially when more than one flautist is present.

While mainly involved in the Jazz scene in the late 1970s, producer Jay Chattaway went on to become a composer for film and television, most notably in many episodes of the *Star Trek* franchises from the early 1990s onwards. Executive producer Bob James is best known in the wider world for his theme to the US TV comedy series *Taxi*, which features his trademark Fender Rhodes playing.

'Montreux Summit' (Bob James) (Vol: 1)

Personnel:

Drums: Billy Cobham, bass: Alphonso Johnson, guitar: Eric Gale, Jeanne Schaffer, Steve Khan, flute: Thijs van Leer, Hubert Laws, Bobbi Humphrey, keyboards: Bob James, George Duke, percussion: Ralph MacDonald, tenor Sax: Benny Golson, Dexter Gordon, Stan Getz, trumpet: Maynard Ferguson, Woody Shaw

This terrific, electrifying, eleven-minute piece – written by Bob James especially for the festival – is tightly arranged and – aside from a lengthy guitar solo, is largely an ensemble track. It's all superbly done, but how much you will enjoy this depends on how much you want this sort of hybrid of modern jazz and fusion, making great use of the sheer size of the ensemble playing, particularly a large, celebrity brass section. Thijs performs largely as part of the ensemble here, but it's terrific.

'Blues March' (Benny Golson) (Vol: 1)

Personnel:

Drums: Billy Cobham, bass: Alphonso Johnson, guitar: Eric Gale, Steve Khan, flute: Thijs van Leer, Hubert Laws, Bobbi Humphrey, piano: George Duke, Bob James percussion: Ralph MacDonald, Tenor Sax: Benny Golson, Dexter Gordon, Stan Getz, trumpet: Maynard Ferguson, Woody Shaw

This is 25-minutes long, and the listener really needs to love jazz soloing to appreciate it, as it's a mid-paced blues with a march-like feel – thus the track title. There's a pace change midway through, but otherwise, it's an opportunity for a variety of the players to show their chops. The fusion angle is dialled down here, to make way for very much a modern jazz feel. There are two flue solos on the piece, but specifically identifying Thijs amongst the ensemble is a challenge!

'Andromeda' (Jay Chattaway) (Vol: 1)
Personnel:
Drums: Billy Cobham, bass: Alphonso Johnson, guitar: Eric Gale, Jeanne Schaffer, Steve Khan, flute: Thijs van Leer, Hubert Laws, Bobbi Humphrey, keyboards: Bob James, George Duke, percussion: Ralph MacDonald, tenor Sax: Benny Golson, Dexter Gordon, Stan Getz, trumpet: Maynard Ferguson, Woody Shaw

This is another side-long piece, but as with the opening track, it's tightly written and performed, with a decent balance of solos and composed ensemble playing. The flutes are there in the mix but do not get any solo spots, which feature both percussionist Ralph MacDonald and drummer Billy Cobham.

'Be Cool' (George Duke) (Vol: 2)
Personnel:
Baritone Saxophone: Bob Militello, bass: Alphonso Johnson, drums: Billy Cobham, electric piano: Bob James, flutes: Bobbi Humphrey, Hubert Laws, Thijs van Leer, keyboards: Eric Gale, George Duke guitar: Steve Khan:: Keyboards, percussion: Ralph MacDonald, trombone: Clifford Hardie, David Horler, Geoffrey Perkins, trumpet: Slide Hampton, Alan Downey, Greg Bowen, Joe Mosello, Stan Mark. synth: Thijs van Leer

This is another great ensemble piece from legendary keyboardist George Duke with an expanded brass section. There are two flute solos – one in the intro and the other mid-track – though neither, sadly, is played by Thijs, who here is involved as part of the flute ensemble and also adding some backup synth. This is one of the strongest tracks on the two albums, full of life and some great playing, particularly Duke's final, electrifying Moog solo.

'**Kanon For Flutes**' (Pachelbel, arranged by Thijs van Leer) (Vol: 2)

Personnel:

Bass: Gordon Johnson, drums: Peter Erskine, electric piano: Bob James, flutes: Bob Militello, Hubert Laws, Thijs van Leer, guitar: Eric Gale, Janne Schaffer, percussion: Ralph MacDonald

Thijs' final contribution is this beautiful arrangement (by Thijs) of a piece by 17th Century German composer Pachebel. Several flutes are featured here, especially when the track moves beyond the written composition into its funky jazz arrangement, but Thijs' contribution is unmistakable, especially his vocalisations during his initial solo. The arrangement for the full band is also by far the most accessible to a jazz-ignorant listener. It's delightful, and Gordon Johnson's bass holds the whole piece together, while Bob James and Eric Gale contribute great solos. Of all the pieces across the two double albums, this is the one that Focus fans should really make a point of hearing on their streaming service of choice. The piece returns to the formal Canon for the final minute, led by Thijs. It's magical.

Introspection 3 – Thijs van Leer

Personnel:

Thijs van Leer: flute

Rogier van Otterloo: conductor

Letty de Jong: voice

Recorded By Dick Bakker

Mixed by Dick Bakker, Joop Niggebrugge

Produced by John J. Vis, Ruud Jacobs

Recorded at the Dureco Studios, Holland

Released September 1977 on CBS records

Highest chart places: Netherlands: 3, UK: did not chart, USA: did not chart

Current edition: BGO CD

It had been two years since Thijs' last introspection album, but with 1977 a much quieter year for Focus, the *Introspection* 'team' of Rogier van Otterloo, John J. Vis, Ruud Jacobs, Letty de Jong and Thijs returned to the studio in the early part of 1977 to record the latest album in the series. This was the last of the *Introspection* albums to be a major success in the Netherlands. While it didn't get to number one as the first two albums had done, on release in September 1977 it rose to number three and stayed on the chart for a remarkable ten months.

In terms of balance, the eight tracks stuck to the formula established on the first two albums. There were five adapted classical pieces, a further sequel to van Otterloo's 'Rondo' sequence, and two van Leer originals, including 'Focus V'. The original version had just been released on *Ship Of Memories* and was accompanied by the often-recorded 'Brother', which had appeared on *O My Love* and was to appear again a few months later on *Focus Con Proby*.

'Reigen Seliger Geister' (Christoph Willibald Gluck)
The album opens with an unusually long piece of the series, 'The Dance Of The Blessed Spirits'. It's a ballet section from 18th Century German composer Gluck's opera *Orfee et Eurydice*, the myth that was also an influence on 'Eruption' of course. It's a stately and poised arrangement and performance, played almost entirely 'straight' with no non-classical affectations. It's a low key but beautiful way to start the album.

'Rondeau' (Henry Purcell)
Conventions are also followed on this fine, if brief, arrangement of English composer Henry Purcell's piece, another Rondo, complete with harpsichord. It's lovely.

'Adagio' (Remo Giazotto, Tommaso Albinoni)
We enter the world of popular classics with this incredibly famous piece – 'Adagio In G Minor' supposedly written by 18th Century Italian composer Tommaso Albinoni, and an 'inspiration' for van Otterloo's 'Rondo' on the original *Introspection* album. Or was it? Italian musicologist Remo Giazotto presented this piece in 1945 as derived from a fragment of a manuscript from the great Italian. However, the fragment was never shown, and it is now generally believed that Giazotto composed it himself, in the style of Albinoni.

The *Introspection* pattern is followed here, with Letty making her first appearance. However, her contribution is tasteful, and Thijs' performance on the flute is wonderful.

'Brother' (Roselie van Leer, Thijs van Leer)
As we discuss elsewhere in this book, the song 'Brother' still awaits its best recording, and this isn't it, either. The orchestra shimmers, Thijs flute takes the main melody line, and Letty – who I would have liked to

121

have heard tackle the song itself, as she had a lovely voice often not best served on these albums – provides backing as do drums, bass, piano and even some subtle lead guitar. Only when the orchestra is allowed to take over with an interlude mid-piece, does the track really come to life. It's a disappointing ending to an otherwise excellent first side. The main melody is still lovely, though.

'Sicilienne' (Gabriel Fauré)

This piece by French composer Faure was originally written in 1983 for orchestra but has also been played as a cello and piano piece. It has fragile melody, played both by flute and the full string ensemble, with Letty's voice sometimes doubling the strings. It's a pleasant opening to side two if a touch overlong at seven minutes.

'Rondo III' (Rogier van Otterloo)

Another of van Otterloo's sprightly 'Rondos' is up next, following the success of the first one in 1972. As usual, it's a mixed – one might even say 'commercial' – arrangement, combining pop instrumentation, flute, Letty (at her most perky and, dare I say it, irritating) and orchestra. It's fun and over very quickly. It's also very, very 'of its time'.

'He Shall Feed His Flock' (Georg Friedrich Händel)

We return to the other side of the *Introspection* coin with this serene and rather charming arrangement of this lesser-known section of Handel's *Messiah*. It's *Jesus* feeding his flock, of course, in a metaphor for Christ as a shepherd. It's a decent choice for the album, and although it's more often sung, this piece's melody works nicely for the flute.

'Focus V' (Thijs van Leer)

We close on this delicate and rather beautiful arrangement of another Focus piece. Thijs' flute takes the main melody initially, with an oboe (always a heart-wrenching instrument) also prominent throughout. The delightful and faintly jazzy main melody is also taken up by Letty (briefly) and the orchestra, and this is a longer version of a track that is over all too quickly on *Ship Of Memories*. The orchestral arrangement is nicely judged and also provides some jazzy touches.

1978 – Did Proby Con Focus?

Focus Con Proby

Personnel:
Thijs van Leer: keyboards, synthesisers, flute
PJ Proby: vocals
Eef Albers: guitar
Philip Catherine: guitar
Bert Ruiter: bass
Steve Smith: drums
Produced by Yde de Jong
Jan van Vrijaldenhoven: engineer
Mike Stavrou: engineer
Recorded: late 1977, released February 1978
Highest chart placings: UK and USA: Did not chart. Netherlands: 27
Available as part of the Focus Hocus Pocus box set and on EMI CD

1977 had been an odd year on the Focus front, with sporadic gigs and
the replacement of Philip Catherine with Eef Albers. The band still had an
album to produce for EMI Holland, and with a lot of his solo instrumental
material squirrelled away for his solo albums, Thijs hit upon the idea to
mix some of the songs he had been working on with Roselie with some
instrumental pieces. Philip Catherine returned to take part in the album,
as was his obligation, having signed the EMI contract, so he shared guitar
duties with Eef. Stand in drummer Richard James – whose funky style was
considered fine for the older material but not for the high concept jazz-
rock that Thijs and Bert had in mind – was not retained. Instead, the duo
brought in American Steve Smith, whose mobile jazz style was much more
in keeping with what they planned. Ironically, Thijs had seen Smith play
at a Dutch festival earlier in 1977 when Smith had been booked to play in
Philip Catherine's band.

The material chosen was five vocal tracks written by Thijs and Roselie
and four instrumentals. Eef Albers brought in two pieces, 'Orion' and
'Night Flight', which the band had already worked up in some of their
sporadic live performances. Philip Catherine's excellent 'Sneezing Bull'
and the Thijs / Bert piece 'Maximum', which dated back to Jan's final
disastrous rehearsals with the band, and had also been played in the Eef
line up that year, were also included. Disappointingly, Philip Catherine's
'Angel Wings' was not considered for the album.

And so we come to the choice of singer. The history of popular music is littered with 'what were they thinking?' moments, and this is certainly one of them. The contact with PJ Proby came via de Jong, who has seen the singer at a club engagement. Despite a good run of hit singles in 1964 and 1965, the American vocalist's career had slumped from then onwards, not helped by his famous 'trouser splitting' routine in early 1965, which saw him arrested for lewdness. There had then followed a decade-long slump, although 1977 had seen his profile increase with a well-publicised attempt to win UK talent show *Opportunity Knocks,* wearing a mask, despite the rule that the show was supposedly for amateur performers. He was later cast as the older (Vegas era) Elvis in the early jukebox show *Elvis The Musical.* Proby left that cast very quickly, however.

The problem seemed to be that, by this time, he was permanently sozzled on whisky. As a result, not only his style of singing – histrionic in the style of the later Elvis – but also his lifestyle, were called into question. However, once Thijs and Bert were convinced that Proby might be able to add something to the songs, both musicians threw themselves into the project with enthusiasm, as did Proby, by all accounts, when he was sober.

The result? It's an undeniably strange listening experience. The marriage of styles, as one might expect, does not work at all, and at times the Proby tracks border on the unlistenable. The album is not helped, despite the high quality of the band's playing, by a distant and unengaging production style. At the same time, Thijs' flute is largely noticeable only by its absence, except on 'Sneezing Bull'. Although fusion had been very much 'in vogue' just before the arrival of punk, this feels like niche music at best and was never going to provide the hit for which the label must have hoped.

Proby believed that he was replacing Jan Akkerman in a sense – his vocals replacing the lyrical nature of Jan's playing. In the hands of a more conventional vocalist, this might indeed have been true, but the histrionic, pseudo-soulful vocalisations of Proby do not do that job. Indeed, any lyricism in the melodies is somewhat repressed by his over-singing. It just doesn't work, and you can tell from the arrangements that the band didn't have a great deal of faith in him. His vocal lines are rarely given a huge amount of space, with Eef often soloing across them, as demonstrated on the opener 'Wingless'.

The album was considered a disaster, and it didn't sell. It's by no means all bad, and it's hard to blame Proby too much. He simply does his 'thing', which – in the main – is completely inappropriate for the material. This makes his contributions hard to listen to, and while there are some good things about all the songs on which he sings, it's hard to imagine that many people would listen to these tracks for true pleasure.

'Wingless' (T. van Leer, R. van Leer)

This is one of the better vocal tracks, and it's not hard to understand why it was chosen as the album opener. Indeed, the first few seconds – a lovely guitar melody and a beautifully jazzy chord progression – are terrific. When the vocals kick in, however, it already becomes apparent that we are in for a bit of a ride. Proby over-sings from the word go, with Eef soloing at the same time across his vocal. Indeed one of the non-vocal issues with the album becomes apparent as well, in that the guitars are just too low in the mix to be effective. This is, after all, a Focus album. However, that guitar melody saves the track, and the playing from the rest of the band is solid, with Thijs contributing Fender Rhodes and string synth – his main weapons of choice at the time. Eef's solo at the end of the song is terrific.

'Orion' (Albers)

The first all-instrumental piece is a showcase for Eef Alber's lead guitar. It's all superbly played, mid-tempo stuff, with some great unison bass work from Bert, but never really rises above its tricky chord structure to become distinctive in any way. As a result, having listened to this piece many times over the years, it always sounds new – which may be a good thing, but it probably isn't. It just hasn't sunk in.

'Night Flight' (Albers)

Eef's second offering is somewhat more impressive, however. This is a frenetic, if brief, jazz fusion piece, with a memorable melody line and, once again, some very impressive playing from Eef, which is not given the most generous of mixes. Steve Smith, so far something of a support player, really comes into his own, with some terrific, mobile playing reminiscent of Billy Cobham. Thijs – largely a support player on the album this far – contributes an interesting synthesiser motif towards the end of the piece with seems out of place but adds some colour nonetheless.

'Eddy' (T. van Leer, R. van Leer)

The second vocal track offers up an interesting comparison with the version of the same song on Thijs' solo album *O My Love*. If that version was somewhat hesitantly sung by Roselie, at least the melody was to the fore. Here's it's given a gospel-style reading, with bluesy soloing from Eef and Thijs on organ and synth bass later in the song. Proby is relatively restrained, which benefits the verses, but unfortunately, he somewhat murders the chorus, over-singing so much the melody is almost buried, and he even wanders off-pitch occasionally. The song itself is still beautiful, however, and would really benefit a treatment from a skilled but more empathic vocalist.

'Sneezing Bull' (Philip Catherine)
Side one closes with this excellent piece – written and largely performed by the Belgian guitarist, with some excellent flute from Thijs. Almost by accident, this really does feel like classic Focus, and it's not hard to understand why it was so quickly adopted as a live piece when Catherine joined the band at the start of 1976. This version is somewhat expanded with the acoustic guitar and flute refrains retained, but with Bert and Steve making a superbly dextrous rhythm section. It's a real shame that this pairing didn't continue beyond this album. On this track, they are superb. Catherine – thus far only on the album as a support musician – also gets to play some rather excellent, echoed lead guitar, duelling with Thijs' flute. Without a doubt, this is the most distinctive and memorable track on the album and really should be on 'Best Of' compilations.

'Brother' (T. van Leer, R. van Leer)
Brace yourselves for another vocal track, albeit with another song with some longevity, remaining in the live repertoire to this day. The piece begins with a lovely neo-classical piano introduction from Thijs, taken from Brahms but also suggesting Barber's 'Adagio For Strings'. The mournful Brahms chord structure remains in place for the song itself, which has Proby's most impressive and appropriate vocal performance. This one actually does suit his voice, and he actually gives it some gravitas, with a percussive delivery which Thijs copies when he sings it 40 to this day. Philip Catherine again provides the lead guitar, and as previously, it's a little more distinctive than Eef's playing elsewhere on the album, including some talkbox work, so fashionable at the time. Proby's singing does get away from him a bit towards the end of the song, but nonetheless, it's not bad.

'Tokyo Rose' (R. van Leer)
There's another lovely introduction to this piece – this time via piano and

an (uncredited) flute from Thijs, and then....disaster strikes. The main part of 'Tokyo Rose' is dreadful, mitigated slightly by an instrumental 'chorus' which more than hints at old school Focus. Those verses, though! Proby raps nonsense, the words partly written by him and partly by Roselie, though Proby himself receives no credit. There may be a proper song in there somewhere, but it's impossible to tell, and even the chorus melody played on guitar with back up from organ and piano loses its appeal the second time around.

'Maximum' (T. van Leer, Ruiter)
This fusion instrumental steadies the ship somewhat, and Catherine takes the lead again, here, as he had done when this piece was first developed during 1976. There are hints of the sort of arrangement that appeared on *Mother Focus* with the band – particularly Bert – playing in a much more funky style. There is plenty of variation from Thijs – especially via a neoclassical electric piano motif and a more expansive use of synthesisers – which give this piece a lot of life. Having said that, at over eight minutes, it really does overstay it's welcome somewhat. There's not really enough going on to maintain even the most patient of listener's interest, and Catherine's soloing – excellent though it is – is too far down in the mix to have the required impact, until a return to the main theme of the piece at the end offers a little excitement. Overall, considering the two years it had been in the live set, the track feels flabby. It's not at all bad, though.

'How Long' (T. van Leer, R. van Leer)
The album closes on one last song, and once again, Proby – unfortunately – kills it with an overwrought vocal. It's really not his fault – he's just the wrong man for the job and the song. This one starts somewhat unexpectedly, with a poppy intro featuring what sounds like an analogue polysynth motif from Thijs. It's breezy and urgent, with some lovely lead guitar from Catherine, but the vocal is just wrong for the song, which in itself is fine, if rather slight. The arrangement is convincing even when it kicks up into a disco-style passage. I rather like this by way of some sonic variation for the album, though I can well imagine many wouldn't have liked the idea that 'Focus had gone disco'. To me, the arrangement is rather charming and works rather well. It's just a shame that the vocal doesn't do it justice. It's quite possible that this piece was earmarked as a single to fit in

with the contemporary disco boom. It's no surprise that this didn't happen, however, and as the last Focus piece to make it on to record for seven or twenty-five years, depending on how you look at it, it's hardly a fitting send-off.

The End?

Author Peet Johnson spends some time asking the question 'why?' concerning *Focus Con Proby,* and with due reason. With the benefit of hindsight, it seems like a crazy decision to record what was to be the last full-band Focus album for twenty-five years in such a manner. Yet, to me, it's an understandable attempt to revive the fortunes of an ailing band. They risked it all with a left-of-centre project, and in the end, they crashed and burned. Sometimes such projects work; sometimes they don't. There's no shame in it.

But with Smith – understandably – not staying with the group, and Thijs – also understandably – showing more interest in his solo career, the band limped on with Richard James back as drummer and Eef Albers as guitarist. The band played its last concert of the 1970s in Terneuzen, Zeeland, in August 1978.

For now, it was all over.

Nice To Have met You – Thijs (Tys) van Leer

Selected Personnel:
Thijs (Tys) van Leer: flute, Oberheim synth
Ralph MacDonald: percussion
Richard Tee: piano and clavinet, organ
Eric Gale: guitar
Anthony Jackson: bass
Harvey Mason: drums
Eef Albers: guitar
Steve Khan: guitar
Tom Scott: tenor saxophone
Randy Brecker: trumpet and flugelhorn
Vivian Cherry, Brenda White, Ken Williams, Gwen Guthrie, Raymond Simpson, Zach Sanders, Bill Eaton: vocals
Produced by Ralph MacDonald and Tom Scott
Engineered by Richard Anderson, assisted by Eddie Heath Jr.
Arrangements by Tom Scott and William Eaton
Recorded at Rosebud Recording, February 1978

Released June 1978
Highest chart placings: UK and USA: Did not chart. Netherlands: 26
Not available on CD, but can be heard on Youtube

Thijs remained signed to CBS as a solo artist, and in November 1977, flew to the USA for meetings and pre-production on his next, non-classical solo album – the connections seemingly made at Montreux that July. Recording began in February 1978. Although Focus Con Proby had only just been re-leased, it is telling that, although unbiased analysts might consider a need to hang around in Europe to promote the new Focus album, he instead chose to jet back to New York to record a new solo record with producers Ralph MacDonald and Tom Scott. Thijs seems to have arrived with, as far as the listener can tell, some excellent instrumental themes, which were then passed over to other arrangers to flesh out into full tracks. They do generally do this in jazz style, with a statement of the main theme and then a series of solos and modulations.

That said, there is little doubt that *Nice To Have Met You* had its eyes or commerciality and the charts. This was an era when many artists – often from the jazz world – were tapping into the interest in club music and the exploding disco scene with crossover albums. While *Nice To Have Met You* is definitely not a disco record as such, there are enough shadows of that idiom to suggest that both CBS and Thijs had their eyes on a major crossover hit, in the same way that Jan we to attempt a year later with 3. Aside from the overall light, jazz-funk vibe, the massed female voices on 'Superffishell' and 'Bahama Mama' have 'chart single' written all over them. It was not to be, of course.

The personnel list, as shown above, is extensive on *Nice To Have Met You,* and it's worth pausing a moment to consider the provenance of most of these artists. Ralph MacDonald, who died in 2011, was a famed New York-based session percussionist and songwriter, with credits that included writing 'Where Is The Love' for Roberta Flack and Donny Hathaway, itself a Grammy winner and also work with Grover Washington Jr. and George Benson. Tom Scott, on the other hand, had even better credentials, as a composer and arranger – he wrote the theme for *Starsky and Hutch* – and as a session sax player. While neither musician was particularly known for their record production skills specifically, Thijs couldn't have been in better hands. The core band that recorded the album was also taken for the New York, African American jazz scene, with, for instance, Richard Tee playing most of the keyboards, Anthony Jackson on bass and Eric Gale on guitar. Two other – white – guitarists are also credited; noted fusion player Steve Khan and the ubiquitous (at the time) Eef Albers. Thijs' playing contributions are largely restricted to flute with a touch of Oberheim synth, while – tellingly – all the album arrangements were handled by Scott or Aretha Franklin's musical director William Eaton. Thijs – himself an excellent arranger, of course – is nowhere to be seen.

Given the cast of thousands involved in the creation of this record, the end result is supremely lightweight. There is very little that would offend anyone (except those with a pathological hatred of jazz-funk), nor is there music to soothe the mind and touch the soul. The Thijs van Leer originals are pretty successful, in the main, though a feeling of mild frustration persists, as with more development rather than these intricate, yet somewhat – er – 'Superffishell' – arrangements, the album might have had more substance to it. It is neither a huge success nor a terrible failure. It is what it is. Thijs' writing for the album – with some help from other composers, including Bert Ruiter, who doesn't appear otherwise – is supremely melodious and competent.

Let us pause for a few other notes before we delve into the music itself. With an eye on the US market, Thijs name was altered to Tys for the record cover (presumably to aid pronunciation in interviews and with radio DJs). The cover, despite the picture on the back, which shows Thijs grinning amongst his 'cast of thousands', has a painting by Richard Hess which screams 'Prog'. This author certainly expected something more like that when he bought the album in (according to the price label) 1981. The back cover also has sleeve notes from one B. Lynn Micale, introducing 'Tys' to an American audience. It didn't work, but it was a nice try. The album has never been released on CD but can be found on Youtube. There's certainly enough here to interest the Focus fan, and a CD release is long overdue.

'My Sweetheart' (van Leer, Akkerman, Ruiter)
Yes, here's the tune from *Mother Focus* given another outing. It starts out a little faster than on that record, but the arrangement here – with its overdubbed flute parts – fails to swing like the Focus version and develops into a jazz-funk flute jam with Thijs riffing around the main melody rather splendidly, it has to be said. As a 'scene-setter' it's fine, with some great piano and wah-wah guitar in sub-disco style. It's all good fun but somewhat inconsequential.

'Nice To Have Met You (Concrete)' (van Leer)
The title track is without doubt the standout piece on the album and might
have made an excellent Focus track. It has a winning flute melody from
Thijs, and the arrangement moves it into high energy fusion territory with a
great guitar solo (probably by Steve Khan) and both horn and string sections
in full flow. The piece is light but beautifully arranged and performed. It
might have made a great TV theme tune – we're in that sort of territory.

'Pastorale' (van Leer)
This is another piece that might have made a decent Focus track, again
written by Thijs, in what was probably intended to be a classical style,
one supposes. The arrangement by Tom Scott is very playful, mixing the
neo-classical with Latin American rhythms to rather clever effect. Harvey
Mason's tight drumming is also worthy of note, and the track – sadly –
fades out just as Thijs is launching into an excellent flute solo.

'Bahama Mama' (A. Johnson)
This is a cover version, albeit a slightly obscure one. It is written by
former Weather Report bassist Alfonso Johnson and appears originally
on his 1977 solo album *Spellbound*. While that version is very much in
the Weather Report-style, its jazzy melody is played on the bass. Here
it's taken by Thijs' flute, of course. It's all a bit forced, with Richard Tee's
funky clavinet to the fore, and the vocal refrain on the chorus – 'Bahama
Mama, I love you' – dates the track somewhat. Seek out the Johnson
version on Youtube, or indeed the *Montreux Summit* live take – for
a better rendition. One wonders what the writer of the piece himself
thought. It's not a great success.

'Hocus Pocus' (van Leer, Akkerman)
Speaking of unsuccessful pieces, this is a pointless jazz-funk reworking of
Focus' most famous song with Thijs' yodelling for all he's worth and Eef
Albers on guitar. Thijs also throws in some speeded up 'Pinky and Perky'
yodelling at one point. It's not too bad, but a bit of a waste of vinyl, when
another van Leer original might have worked far, far better. However,
one suspects that this track was intended to give the album some sort of
commercial focal point. It doesn't work.

'Tonight Beneath The Sky' (T. van Leer, R. van Leer)
This is a more successful effort. Again, it's a lightweight, percussion-laden

arrangement of a piece that might have made a fine Focus piece with more development. Thijs' overdubbed flutes are very effective, and the Latin flavour of the track certainly works in context.

'Rosebud' (van Leer)

With a very different tone to its first few bars, it seems that we are going to get something a little different, here. However, the piece soon settles down into a string-laden slice of easy listening, with more than a few hints of Bach in Thijs' main flute melody. Again, there's enough here to suggest than a more sympathetic arrangement might have produced more interesting results, but this is light as a feather and actually overstays it's welcome in this arrangement at slightly less than five minutes.

The piece is presumably named both for the New York studio at which the album was recorded and for Roselie, Thijs' then-wife.

'Super Ffishell' (van Leer, B. Ruiter, W.Eaton)

The album closes on a jaunty note with this funky number with more massed female vocals singing the refrain – a play on words, using the name of the then-CBS executive Jim Fishel. Tee plays some great organ and Tom Scott gets a tenor sax solo, but again we are in 'funky jam' territory, as the ladies sing:

> Well alright, he's Super Ffishell
> He's moving out at midnight
> He's living on the faultline
> Yea, Super Ffishell

It's hardly Bob Dylan. Arranger William Eaton contributed enough to the piece to get a writing credit, although the track was originally deleveoped by Thijs and Bert Ruiter. Apart from some flute soloing a little low in the mix, Thijs hardly features.

Aranjuez – Jan Akkerman

Personnel:
Jan Akkerman: guitar
Claus Ogerman: arrangements, conducting
Niels-Henning Ørsted Pedersen: bass
Jan Schuurman: engineer (guitar dubbing)
Joop Niggebrugge, Pieter Nieboer: engineer (mixdown)

Dick Lowzey: engineer (recording)
John J. Vis, Ruud Jacobs: production
Released: March 1978
Highest chart placings: Netherlands: 20, UK: Did not chart. USA: Did not chart
Current edition: CD on BGO records, or remastered as part of the *Complete Jan Akkerman* box set

Jan has had some harsh words to say about Thijs' *Introspection* series, the implication being that the flautist had appropriated popular classical composers like Bach for purely commercial, rather than artistic purposes. This is probably harsh. There is no doubting the 'popular' appeal of the *Introspection* series, as their commercial success showed. Jan, on the other hand, claimed that his choice of pieces and his arrangements for 1978's *Aranjuez* came from an emotional place; the guitarist wanted to do real justice to the legacy of composers like Rodrigo and Villa-Lobos. He said, in Dutch *Melody Maker* in 1985:

> I made music from my heart, very emotionally. No Bach or Beethoven, but Villa Lobos and composers like that. And in fact, I used a rock guitar, a Les Paul Gold Top, but it sounds very acoustic... I've worked five months on that record, without a conductor; purely feelings. I heard the orchestra in the back of my mind and, I thought, I'll try to find a way through that.

On the surface, there are a fair few similarities to the *Introspection* albums. Here we have a lead instrument sitting against some lush orchestral arrangements, playing tunes that will be familiar to many. But Jan has a point. Although the orchestral arrangements are bold, the album is shorn of the rather cheesy bells and whistles that have prevented Thijs' albums from ageing too well. Indeed, the spectre of 'jazz' lurks in every corner of this album, both in Jan's clean and delicate playing and in the way that Claus Ogerman's arrangements often shimmer with a jazz aesthetic, suggesting Mancini as much as Mantovani.

The 'trick' – if it is one – of using a Les Paul to play classical music works beautifully here. The electric guitar, played cleanly and without distortion, can never rival its classical or Spanish siblings in a harmonic battle, yet Jan's electric allows him to mix up the lyrical, sensitive side of his playing with some delightfully jazzy runs. For a few years at the end of the 1970s, there was a fashion for using the electric guitar in classically-styled music. See, for instance, John William's work on the first few Sky albums, or the two orchestral pieces that Yes' Steve Howe recorded in the famous Studio Three at Abbey Road in London for his 1979 solo record *The Steve Howe Album.* Along with a piece composed by Howe himself, he also recorded part of Vivaldi's *Lute Concerto in D.* It is no coincidence that Howe also used a Gibson Les Paul for these sessions. Tonally, it works perfectly alongside an orchestra.

The choice of well known German composer/arranger Claus Ogerman to join Jan on the project was crucial. Ogerman, who died in 2016, had worked with artists as diverse as Billy Holliday, Solomon Burke and jazz maestro Bill Evans but also had many jazz-tinged classical compostions to his name. He couldn't have been a more perfect choice. Special praise should also go to Norwegian stand-up bassist Niels-Henning Ørsted Pedersen for some sympathetic and well-judged playing – the only named artist outside of the orchestra.

Nonetheless, the album is something of a white elephant. Despite the hard and credible work of both Jan and Claus Ogerman, the album had nothing like the success of Thijs' albums with van Otterloo, and Jan did not try that path again. If the album has a fault, it's one that also discredits Thijs' albums, up to a point. The orchestral arrangements are too lush and violin-dominated to have aged as well as they might have. Higher-register strings and woodwind are prominent; perhaps too prominent. Furthermore, it's an incredibly one-paced album. Many of the melodies are lovely, but by the second half of the second side – and a pleasing rendition of the Focus classic 'Love Remembered' – the listener really starts to feel a sense of déjà vu, despite the tracks themselves, taken on their own merits, hitting the mark. However, on its own terms, the album remains an artistic success and is well worth a listen.

'Adagio From Concierto De Aranjuez' (Joaquin Rodrigo)

Why not grab them with the 'hit' first? This piece is, of course, one of the most famous tunes in the classical repertoire. This version is lush and Jan's electric guitar, beautifully played though it is, does mean that the track loses some of it's famous 'Spanish' texture. However, it's an excellent start, and Ogerman's orchestration does hint at jazz far more than Rodrigo's original. As a result, it's an intriguing beginning, setting a tone that the rest of the album will follow.

'Nightwings' (Claus Ogerman)

Jan and Claus have one composition each here, and this is Ogerman's. It begins with a shimmering orchestral introduction before moving into lyrical jazz territory. Jan's guitar takes up the main, jazzy theme, with fine accompaniment from the Norwegian bassist. It's all rather charming, with the atmosphere of a movie love theme, until Jan thrills with some icy, dextrous runs, which prevent the piece from falling into the cliché that prevents some of the Introspection pieces from working as well as they might.

'Modinha (Prelúdio)' (Heitor Villa-Lobos)

This is the first of three pieces composed by Brazilian maestro Heitor Villa-Lobos. Villa-Lobos, who died in 1959, is generally considered to be the best-known South American composer. As well as cello and guitar, he also conducted and was a prolific composer. That Jan chose the music of this man – hardly a household name outside the America's – is a testament to Akkerman's emotional attachment to the project.

Maintaining the sensitive, slow pace of the album thus far, this again begins with a delightful string arrangement and a lovely guitar melody, before the orchestra largely takes over with solo violin also to the fore. It's a slight piece, however, with Jan's talents somewhat subdued.

'Españoleta' (Gaspar Sanz)

We head slightly up-tempo, but back in time, with this piece from 17th Century Spanish composer Gaspar Sanz. Here, Jan begins by playing the melody using the bass strings on his guitar, before moving up an octave. The melody itself feels timeless as a result of the arrangement, although it certainly has an aura of church music about it. It's well-chosen, and a faster section just before the end works nicely.

'Pavane Pour Une Infante Defunte' (Maurice Ravel)

To France this time, and the work of famed early 20th-century composer Ravel, best known, of course, for his 'Bolero'. Here, the tone is slow and sedate, with the orchestral arrangement busier than Jan's guitar. Indeed, the arrangement is a little overdone and almost hysterical in places, despite a pleasant flute interlude. One suspects that had the orchestra been less busy, Jan might have been allowed to play his melody line a little faster, and the overall piece might have been more of a success. In the end, the main melody remains elusive, and while the piece is full of romanticism, it's not especially successful overall.

'Love Remembered' (Jan Akkerman)

This one will fascinate Focus fans. It's a complete rearrangement of one of Jan's favourite pieces, 'Love Remembered' from *Focus 3*. Again, the piece is taken deathly slow, with a jazzy orchestral arrangement. However, on this occasion, Jan's melody line and embellishments are recognisable and well-performed, and when the strings take up the melody, it really works. Its slower pace will not please some Focus fans, but here the melody carries the piece through to a satisfying conclusion.

'The Seed Of God (From "Magdalena")' (Heitor Villa-Lobos)

The album finishes on two more pieces from Villa-Lobos, and this first features another sweet, lush arrangement from Ogerman, and a fine and sensitive performance from Jan, a good lead melody and some expertly played embellishments. It's very much 'as you were' until an astonishing lead run from Jan just before the close.

'Bachianas Brasileiras No 5' (Heitor Villa-Lobos)

The album is at its best when the orchestral arrangement strays a little from lush romanticism, as it does here, with something a touch more surreal, modern and challenging — a little more Holst and a little less Nelson Riddle. With Jan's guitar supporting and playing something a little more interesting than just a straight melody line, this is possibly the most challenging and progressive piece on the album. It's an odd but excellent end to the record.

Jan Akkerman – Live – Jan Akkerman

Personnel:
Cees van Der Laarse: bass
Bruno Castelucci: drums
Jan Akkerman: guitar
Jasper van't Hof, Willem Ennes: keyboards
Neppie Noya: percussion
Tom Barlage: saxophone, keyboards
David Richards: engineer
Jan Schuurman, Richard Debois: mixing
Joop Niggebrugge: mastering
Recorded July 7, 1978, at the Montreux Jazz Festival by the Mountain Recording Studios
Mixed August/September 1978 at the Soundpush Studios, Blaricum, Holland

Released: January 1979
Highest chart placings: Netherlands: 40, UK: did not chart. USA: did not chart
Current edition: remastered CD as part of *Complete Jan Akkerman* box set

If *Aranjuez* can be construed as a one-off project, then it was back to Jan's
intended 'day job' for an appearance on 7 July 1978 at the Montreux Jazz
Festival, at which Thijs had played the year before. This album is a record
of that performance, with a live band based around the one that had
played on his 1977 solo album. There was no Pierre, one should note,
with Bruno Castellucci on drums and old cohort Tom Barlage on sax,
while Willem Ennes joined Jasper van't Hoff on the keys.

This is certainly Jan, the Jazzman. Even the choice of cover tells us this,
with Jan photographed in movement, wearing a leather jacket and playing
the sort of Gibson more often associated with jazz. Everything is kept
modest and simple, as it should be. Richard DuBois, who helmed *Eli*, and
Jan's first proper solo album, returned in the producer's chair.

It's a good set. Despite the lack of vocals, the show feels very much like
a 'journey', with tracks leading logically from one to another. There are
even two Focus tracks (although 'Crackers' was only given to the band
grudgingly, of course), and both fit seamlessly into the album's 'narrative'.
That it's a short record at little more than 34 minutes (and contains two
drum solos) might not feel like value for money, but it certainly helps
build a vibe.

'Transitory' (van't Hoff)
This is very much an introductory, ambient piece, dominated by rich,
sensuous keyboards, sax and Neppie Noya's percussion flurries, segueing
straight into:

'Skydancer' (Akkerman)
An opening flurry of notes from Jan introduces this atmospheric piece
from Jan's 1977 solo album. It's as good as the version on the original
album, with Tom Barlage's soprano sax acting as a counterpoint to Jan's
guitar motif, with its distinctive chord progression; part classics, part jazz.
When the band transition into pure fusion, it's breathtaking. Indeed,
some of the chord progressions are pure Focus here. The jam section is
much funkier in this version, with guitar and synth trading licks. A drum
solo is expertly performed and very 'Montreux,' but rather unfortunate,
actually puncturing the expertly crafted atmosphere somewhat.

'Pavane' (Akkerman)

We slow down with the tense atmospheric build of 'Pavane', also from the 1977 album, both brooding and powerful. As with the album version, it's all about subtle shifts in tone (and occasionally, key) rather than overt virtuosity, and it works, even if at times it does cry out for a vocalist!

'Crackers' (Akkerman)

We leap in pace with this extended version of 'Crackers'. The 'talkbox' motif of the Focus version is gone, so the melody is carried in more subtle ways, making this rendition rather more of a 'groove' than its more 'in your face' Focus cousin. When Jan solos, he dazzles with some breathtaking runs which, nonetheless, mirror the jazzy chord progression perfectly. Cees van der Laarse's bass line sneaks very close to disco at one point, and there certainly is a danceable quality, that is infectious. A breezy Fender Rhodes solo gets a round of applause from the audience, and there's a drum and percussion duet that breaks up the flow completely, though the audience seem appreciative, and it leads into:

'Tommy' (Barlage)

Jan delivers this classic solo pretty much 'as written' though with less feedback and more sax, before developing into an extended jam, with Barlage's sax to the fore, albeit a little low in the mix. This also segues directly into:

'Azimuth' (L.M. Biljsma)

This cover version is a funky jazz/soul workout with an excellent, fluid solo from Jan and (if I am not much mistaken) some rhythm guitar overdubs. It ends with a reprise of 'Skydancer' and the show ends. Again, it's impressive stuff. The band is tight, and Jan is in fine form.

1979 – End Of An Era

1979 dawned with Focus as a band seemingly over and both Thijs and Jan concentrating on their solo careers. Bert joined Dutch proggers Earth and Fire in 1978, which also featured his partner Jerney Kaagman, and stayed until 1990, although they disbanded for four years in the mid-80s.

Changing musical tastes in society also saw a shifting in the solo fortunes of both Thijs and Jan. The former's *Introspection* series was already starting to date, and his outing in 1979 was to be the last in the series for the time being. Jan tried – as many jazz and pop artists tried to do around that time – to embrace music that fit in with the disco craze, with moderate success. As the 1970s became the 1980s, both musicians found themselves marginalised and in need of new directions and new collaborations. But in 1979, both had new albums to assess.

Introspection 4 – Thijs van Leer
Personnel:

Thijs van Leer: flute, keyboards
Rogier van Otterloo: arrangements. conductor
Dick Bakker, Emile Elsen, Joop Niggebrugge: mixing
John J. Vis, Ruud Jacobs: production
Emile Elsen: recording engineer
Letty de Jong: vocals
Released in CBS on 1979
Current edition: BGO CD (out of print). Available on Youtube.

This was to be the last album of the *Introspection* sequence. While the first three records had been massive successes, times they were a changin' and the formula was no longer as successful as it had once been. By comparison with the first three, the album was a flop, only reaching sixteen in the Dutch charts and hanging around for a relatively modest thirteen weeks.

However, *Introspection IV* stuck to the existing formula for now. The pieces were generally shorter than on volume three, with a trio of original compositions from Thijs, two of which were to have lives beyond this series. 'Song For Eva' – presumably written as a possible Focus piece, since it's writing credit here includes Bert, although it was written for Thijs' daughter Eva – was not to appear in a rock arrangement until it was demoed by the short-lived Eef Albers line up in 1995, and finally appeared

on the *Focus Family Album* in 2017, in a lengthy, bluesy arrangement.
Interestingly, by the time it appeared on these later recordings, Bert's
writing credit had disappeared. 'Le Tango' was to have two further
versions; firstly on the Thijs / Jan reunion album *Focus* of 1985, to be
discussed shortly, and then on the Focus album *X* as 'Birds Come Fly Over
(Le Tango)' in 2012.

'Arcangelo (Gigue From Sonata Op. 5 No. 9)' (Arcangelo Corelli)
This is as bright an opening as any of the *Introspection* series, a
delightfully perky Baroque piece by Italian composer Arcangelo Corelli,
originally written for the violin. It's short but rather splendid.

'Introspection 4' (Rogier van Otterloo)
Although there's no 'Rondo' on this album, Rogier Otterloo does present
one composition, a lyrical and gently pleasing piece with Thijs' flute
accompanied largely by piano, bass, drums, horns and Letty's vocals, quite
low in the mix. It's certainly pleasant, but the melody – which strives to
tug at the heartstrings – is a little too syrupy to have stood the test of time.
It's the sort of tune that cries out for a lead vocal rather than flute, but as
it is, the track feels incredibly unchallenging and middle of the road.

'Rondeau Des Enfants' (Thijs van Leer)
The first of three pieces composed by Thijs', this *is* a rondo, and it feels
very authentic, though the atmosphere is somewhat punctuated by Letty's
vocals, which the piece could have done without. Otherwise, it's a very
enjoyable track.

'Grave, Allegro, Adagio, Allegro (Sonate In E Minor)' (Georg Friedrich Händel)
We return to the 17th century for this stately piece (or series of pieces, as
it's part of a sonata) by Handel, which was written especially for flute.
The track runs through several different short movements (thus the
title), allowing Thijs to really show off his technique in a way he is rarely
allowed to do, even on these easy-listening albums. It's superbly played.

'Le Tango' (Roselie van Leer, Thijs van Leer)
To end side one, we have one of several versions of 'Le Tango' that have
appeared with Thijs' name attached to them over the years – we'll look

at another in the next chapter. This is – by far – the best. Although rather moving away from the *Introspection* formula of lush orchestration, It's full of drama and tension in its main verse before becoming something entirely different with a bright and breezy middle section, while Letty's vocals work nicely when the piece returns to the slow, sensual early iteration. Given that there are ten pieces on this album, this one actually feels too short, if anything.

'Air' (Georg Philipp Telemann)
We return to the Baroque period in terms of composition, but not arrangement with the first track on side two, written by German composer Telemann. Rogier's arrangement places this piece squarely within the *Introspection* formula, with only hints of its 17th Century origins and a lush orchestral arrangement. It can perhaps be argued that the formula was tiring at this point, which might explain why, relatively speaking, there is so much variation on this album.

'Pastorale' (Domenico Scarlatti)
It's back to Italy, but still the Baroque period, for this bright piece by Scarlatti, ideally suited to the flute. Rogier's orchestral arrangement works nicely, enhancing the period flavour, and as usual, Thijs' playing is immaculate.

'Largo E Dolce' (Johann Sebastian Bach)
It is fitting that the final album in this sequence should include a piece by Thijs' beloved J.S. Bach, and here it is. It's probably not one of the composer's most memorable melodies, but the arrangement is sympathetic and the playing immaculate.

'Siciliano, Allegro' (Georg Friedrich Händel)
It's back to Handel for these further two pieces. They were originally written for recorder, but a quick sprint around Youtube shows how ubiquitous this piece is for music grade exams, including for trumpet and saxophone. Rogier's arrangement gives both sections rather more studied elegance than is often the case with this piece. It's very nicely done.

'Song For Eva' (Bert Ruiter, Thijs van Leer)
We close on this piece written for Thijs' daughter. Clearly, it was originally created as a Focus piece, particularly as Bert has a writing credit. It was

eventually to become a Focus track, of course, on the Focus Family Album. It's a glorious melody, and it's a desperate shame that a version was never recorded with Jan. The orchestral arrangement has a touch of jazz about it, and again the pop sensibilities of the piece mean that Letty's vocals are welcome rather than a distraction. It's a beautiful, relaxing way to finish the album and indeed the series as a whole.

3 – Jan Akkerman

Selected Personnel:
Jan Akkerman: guitars
Peter Schon: keyboards
Gene Sontini: bass
Bruno Castellucci: drums
Neppie Noya: percussion on 'She's So Divine'
Duane Hitchings: keyboards
Bunny Brunell: bass
David Igelfeld: drums:
Yvette Cason: vocals on 'Funk Me'
Willie Dee: vocals on 'She's So Divine'
Jay Denson: engineer (Netherlands)
Neal Teeman: engineer (New York)
Dick Lewis: engineer (London)
Jan Akkerman and Richard DeBois: mixing
Richard DeBois: producer
Highest chart placings: Did not chart in any territory
Current edition: Wounded Bird CD or part of Complete Jan Akkerman box set

Jan had spent most of the 1970s trying on genres for size. However, 1979 was to see him take these explorations to their furthest extreme. 3 sees Jan dipping his toe into the waters of American-style jazz-funk, in the same way that Thijs had done the previous year. The cover says it all, with a while-suited Jan superimposed on an expanse of water. He's casting a shadow – it's an acoustic guitar. Get it? This design is very much 'of its time', though it's hard to imagine anyone thinking it to be a piece of high art even in 1979.

The whole album feels like it was conceived and recorded on the west coast of the USA, but in fact – considering that Jan was not a great fan or air travel – it was mainly a Dutch affair, with backing tracks recorded in the Netherlands and only the more specialised instruments, for instance, the horns, vocals and strings, recorded further afield, in New York and London. Mixing took place in sunny California, with Jan involved, so presumably, a plane flight had to be endured in the end. In the main, however, this is a record created to achieve a vibe, with Jan keeping his virtuosity largely in the locker. Indeed, for much of the album, he feels like he's desperate to be George Benson. His playing – on what sounds like a hollow-bodied Gibson – is tasteful, expertly done and well recorded, but aside from the odd lightning-fast run, he could be anyone.

That's not to say that the album doesn't have plenty of merits. I have a soft spot for this type of cool jazz-funk, and while the record does tread something of a fine line between fashionable dance music and easy listening, it's well done. Both the vocal tracks are decent songs, and while the US influence is somewhat overpowering, on its own terms, it's a musical success, with a warm production, some great playing from Jan's core band, and some terrific horn arrangements.

However, released on Atlantic again and given a reasonably high profile at the time, it flopped. Indeed, it's hard to know who it was aimed at. Many of Jan's Focus audience wouldn't have liked it, and there's not quite enough jazz for the jazz fans. One saving grace, however, is how funky it is. It really doesn't sound like a bunch of Dutch guys.

'Stingray (Get Up With That)' (Akkerman / Castellucci)
The album begins as it means to go on with this pleasant tune – as dominated by Peter Schon's keyboards as it is by Jan's guitar. Jan chugs away engagingly, high in the mix, but his parts early in the song could be played by anyone. Later in the tune he does add to the groove with some effective, funky chordal work, not unlike George Benson, and four minutes in, he lets loose with a rapid, tasteful and annoyingly short solo. As for the rest of the arrangement – it's dominated by some well arranged and judged strings, horns and solo flute. It's all very nicely done, but very much 'of its time'. It's not hard to imagine it being played in some sort of fantasy London disco circa 1979.

'Wait And See' (Akkerman)
This is rather better, at least in the beginning. It's a much jazzier tune, very reminiscent of Jan's writing style, even if it's Schon's keyboards and those pesky horns and strings that once again dominate, rather than Jan's guitar. Here he contributes some excellent, if restrained, work

putting his volume control skills to good use. However, he does seem to be fighting with Schon's (albeit lovely) piano. The schmaltz is turned up to the max with less than a minute to go, with a swirl of strings that smacks of easy listening at its worst, and the song fades out just as it might be regaining its footing. It's a partial success.

'She's So Divine' (Bernard Oattes, Rob van Schaik)

Aha! A vocal track, and a cover version at that, written by contemporary Dutch pop duo Bernard Oattes and Rob van Schaik. This is a slice of late 70s soul / funk with Jan again in George Benson style, and lead vocals by US session man Billy Dee (who was later to turn up as a member of Gary Moore's band G Force). It's actually rather good, with female backing vocals on the chorus as one might expect on what was presumably considered 'the single.' Dee's lead vocal is excellent, if hardly distinctive. As for Jan, he contributes one well-judged solo mid-song, but otherwise – once again – it might be anyone playing the guitar parts. My goodness, it's a long way from Focus, though.

'Funk Me' (Akkerman, Yvette Cason)

Side two kicks off with another vocal track, with a lead vocal performed this time by Yvette Cason, an American vocalist and actress who provides the lyrics. She can certainly sing, and this is an excellent piece of very funky soul, possibly the most impressive track on the album within its own stylistic constraints. Jim Odgren's alto sax solo is also excellent. Jan is largely absent, though, apart from some choppy rhythm guitar, until he contributes an effective, bluesy solo midway though the song. It's all good stuff, but again, it hardly shows off how distinctive a guitarist he can be.

'This Is The One' (Akkerman, M.Gibbs)

Now, this is pretty decent. Whereas some of the pieces here veer very close to easy listening, this track is as funky as anything from George Clinton and Funkadelic, and the horn arrangement is terrific. Jan's weapon of choice here is the talkbox, and it's a nice texture on a track that is otherwise dominated by some great bass playing and some cultured synth. There's a brief Benson-esque solo towards the end, but as with the rest of the album, Jan is playing within himself, letting the arrangements do the talking. Overall, this is terrific fun – you can almost hear it on the soundtrack to a late 1970s cop show.

'Nightprayer' (Akkerman)

This is a much smoother, slower tune, as the funk is toned down in favour of a more subtle, atmospheric arrangement. And – joy of joys – Jan dominates this one with some tasteful and well-judged soloing throughout. There's a mournful, sad feel to the chord structure that hints at classical music. Indeed, despite the late-night, jazzy vibe (there's a lovely jazz piano solo halfway through) and the excess of both horn and string arrangements, it's just possible to imagine this in an altered form on a Focus album. Jan has his best moment just before the fade-out – with a spine-tingling run. It's a lovely end to the album proper.

'Time Out Of Mind' (Akkerman)

The album closes on an odd note – almost literally. This is a piece of very brief electronica, accompanied (at the start) by a lightning-fast guitar run. At barely a minute, one wonders why it's there at all.

What Happened Next

As the 1980s began, both Thijs and Jan must have felt marginalised –
dinosaurs in fact – despite neither being much over 30. While the golden
age of progressive rock still had a few twitches of life left in it, a new
breed were taking over, and for both artists, pickings were to be slim for
many years. Even so, neither were to be strangers to the charts – if only
in the Netherlands. In 1981, Jan had a minor hit with a middle-eastern,
dance-flavoured track called 'Oil In The Family' – a satirical comment, one
suspects, on the domination of the Middle East states over the oil industry
– and produced the album of the same name in two days flat.

Meanwhile, although the relatively poor chart showing of *Introspection
4* had put paid to that series until a one-album revival in 1992, Thijs
exploration of the popular classics for the flute continued, often with
Rogier van Otterloo in tow. In 1980, an album called *Collage* featured a
version of Ravel's 'Bolero', then popularised in the Blake Edwards movie
10 starring Bo Derek and Dudley Moore. Indeed, an early version of that
album had a sexy picture of Mrs Derek on the cover, a shameless but
understandable promotional tactic. Another album *Reflections* followed in
1981. Thijs also made a more contemporary move into sacred music with
the exquisite one-off Pedal Point project and that international band's
double album *Dona Nobis Pacem*.

In short, both men continued their solo careers to waning, but
nonetheless still considerable, public interest. However, the spectre of
Focus remained, and 'what might have been' hung over both careers.
Could Focus be revived in any shape at all? It turned out that it could.

Focus – Jan Akkerman and Thijs van Leer (1985)
Personnel:
Thijs van Leer: keyboards, flute, vocals
Jan Akkerman: guitar, guitar synthesisers, bass, keyboards
Tato Gomez: bass on 'Russian Roulette'
Ruud Jacobs: big bass on 'Beethoven's Revenge'
Sergio Castillo: drum fills on 'Le Tango'
Usted Zamir Ahmad Khan: tabla on 'Indian Summer'
Produced by Ruud Jacobs
Co-produced by Thijs van leer, Jan Akkerman and Theo Balijon
Recorded at Studio Spitzbergen, Zuidbroek
Mixed by Emile Elsen, Jan Akkerman and Theo Balijon at Dureco Studio, Weep

Released in 1985 on Mercury Records in the USA, Vertigo in Europe.
Highest chart place: Netherlands: 33. UK: Did not chart, USA: Did not chart
Current edition: Music On CD, CD and part of Red Bullet *Focus Hocus Pocus Box*

While this album technically falls outside the scope of a book about Focus
in the 1970s, I hope the reader will allow a little poetic licence here, as
this album, in some ways, completes our story. It certainly marks the end
of any sort of creative collaboration between our two 'heroes', save for a
few live performances of 'the hits'.

The initiative for the album came from Jan's management, Willem
Goebel and Timo van der Brink, who pitched the idea to the two
musicians. With labels Mercury and Vertigo on board (Phonogram
had initially had wanted a 'greatest hits' album with the fashionable
Trevor Horn producing), writing and rehearsals began in earnest, with
Thijs – in particular – throwing everything he had into what must have
been considered a 'make or break' project. The album was initially
to be produced by Thijs, Jan and engineer Theo Balijon, but with the
project taking an age and seeing no signs of coming to an end, Thijs' old
collaborator Ruud Jacobs was brought in to hurry things along and get
the album finished – for as little cash as possible. According to Balijon,
this amplified any tension between Thijs and Jan, and it's possible that
the hurry to get the album completed left such a bad taste in both their
mouths that it poisoned any possibility that they might work together
again. This, despite the relative mediocrity of the album itself, is a
desperate shame.

The album was finally recorded in earnest over a six week period
in April and May 1984 at Studio Spitsbergen, Zuidbroek, but was not
released for almost a year, where it appeared at a desperately poor 33 on
the Dutch charts and stayed for only the one week, before disappearing
without a trace. It bombed in all other territories. Musicians often blame
their labels for lack of promotion, often without justification. However,
here such a charge does seem to be plausaible, with the label pretty much
ignoring it. The length of time that the album 'remained in the can' says it
all, really. This author bought it on vinyl at the time of release in the UK,
so its distribution at least must have been adequate!

The sonic constraints of two sides of vinyl led to two tracks being
heavily edited 'Beethoven's Revenge' and 'Who's Calling'. The CD version
of the album restores both these tracks to their full length, for better
or worse. Indeed, from the writing sessions, the two picked around

twelve pieces for inclusion, with Ruud Jacobs making the final decision regarding tracks and mixes, a situation which neither Thijs nor Jan found satisfactory.

The resulting album is something of a mixed bag. There are some terrific pieces and even some excellent moments in otherwise over-extended tracks. The performances are good, and some of the synthesisier arrangements show a lot of invention, even if it is in a losing cause. Both men play their hearts out. But the album had dated very badly, particularly in its use of the then-modern synth patches and the non-human Linn drum machine. The fact that Linn drums were used is something of a red herring in terms of quality, since most real drummers sounded like this in the 1980s anyway, and the issue is less about whether the drums are played by a human or a machine, but what pattern they are beating out in the first place. Here the quirks – and indeed the fills – of a van der Linden or even a Kemper are badly missed.

A band consisting of Thijs, Tato Gomez and drummer Mario Argandona (both members of Thijs' then band Pedal Point) played some live concerts with Jan guesting in April and then the four played a few concerts as 'Focus' in May 1985. Other gigs were considered but then dropped when the album failed to sell. And that was it.

'Russian Roulette' (van Leer)
On the face of it, 'Russian Roulette' is quite a decent start. A strong guitar melody has hints of 'Focus IV' about it and Jan's playing is expressive. The tempo change also works nicely, in true Focus style, and Thijs' piano work is also lovely if a touch 'digital' sounding. What causes the alarm bells to ring immediately are the heavy synth pads and the sound of the Linn drums. The track seems to have two sections that follow each other and don't develop, so while it's a perfectly decent start, at the point that the track fades out, the listener is not left begging for more.

'King Kong' (Akkerman)
Ah, this is more like it! Jan's tune is delightfully original, with the first appearance of Thijs' happy, dancing flute, and Jan in the main providing a counterpoint on acoustic guitar. The Linn drums provide percussive interjections without being intrusive, and the melody is excellent. The handclaps are also an unusual and welcome touch. This is true Focus and something of a lost gem. The mix is light and has more warmth than this album is usually credited for. It's delightfully short, too.

'Le Tango' (van leer, Roselie Peters)

Oh, dear. 'Le Tango' might have had some promise had it received a more simple arrangement, but here it's just a vehicle for synth and Linn drum effects, and it's a bit of a trial. The issue is not in the writing, but in the arrangement, which had probably dated even before the album was released. Jan's solo midway through the track is excellent but so buried in effects that it's hard to pull it out from the wall of sound. The version on *Introspection 4* is much better. Drummer Sergio Castillo played an electronic kit during recording, but only his fills were retained in the final mix.

'Indian Summer' (Akkerman)

This is rather more interesting, however, and Jan and Thijs' synth patterns actually work very well, having dated rather less badly than much of the rest of the album. Indeed, there's more than a hint of 1970s electronica with a touch of Weather Report about this piece. Tato Gomez provides some excellent slap bass and Ustad Zamar Ahmad Khan's tabla is also a nice touch. Jan throws in some brief acoustic flurries, and Thijs also solos effectively on flute, using that instruments lower register. Overall, this is rather good, and the offbeat Linn drum rhythm works well.

'Beethoven's Revenge (Bach-One-Turbo-Overdrive)' (Akkerman)

Let's dance! Ok, let's not. So ubiquitous is the Linn drum on this one that whatever else happens is barely noticed. The track has some good moments, both in its ten and in its eighteen-minute versions, particularly some great, rhythmic playing from Jan (though, again, laden in synth effects) and some lovely flute tones from Thijs. But the whole track feels like a dance remix of something a bit more interesting. One can hear the Beethoven, but where Canadian rock band Bachman Turner Overdrive fits in is hard to work out. Check out Jan's reinterpretations of this piece on his *Heartware* and particularly *The Noise Of Art* albums. Despite the huge amount of craft going on here as the track develops into a well-played jam, this is almost unlistenable now.

'Ole Judy' (van Leer)

This track certainly has hints of 'old' Focus, due to some recognisable and less effects-laden lead work from Jan (which is his best work on the album) and some old school over-blown flute from Thijs. The heavy

synths and Linn drums set it apart, however, and while this is actually
quite decent, it's VERY 1980s.

'Who's Calling' (Akkerman / van Leer)

As a four-minute album closer, with its stately synth pattern and neo-
classical flute and lead guitar passages, this might have been a fitting album
coda. But, once again, an initial idea is taken and stretched without overdue
development. As a result, this piece is too ponderous and over-inflated to
work in either it's seven or (count em) sixteen-minute iterations. Again, it's
nicely written and performed but just goes on for too long without offering
much apart from almost casual vamping from both men.

Reunions And The New Focus

Thijs and Jan have never worked creatively since the recording of *Focus*.
However, there have been further reunions of one kind or another. On
20 April 1990, Jan, Thijs, Bert and Pierre reconvened for a short, one-off
performance as part of Radio Veronica's 'Goud Van Oud' TV special at the
Americahal in Apeldoorn. The initiative for the appearance came from
Jan, as a 'present' to TV producer Frans Meijer and his manager Martin
Eisma. Their 23-minute set was 'Focus III', 'Focus II', 'House Of The King',
'Sylvia' (with a new intro from Jan), 'Tommy' and 'Hocus Pocus'. While
the set is excellent, and everyone seems to be having a good time except
a rather serious-looking Bert, it's clear from the footage included in the
Focus 50 Years Anthology DVD that there's almost no communication
between Jan and Thijs. Having said that, given their positions on the huge
stage, that would have been difficult anyway.

A few weeks later, the band – without Jan – also mimed to 'House
Of The King' on television. Jan had been invited but turned down the
appearance, even when that track replaced the planned 'Hocus Pocus', a
piece with which Jan had fallen out of love, which Thijs knew. It seemed
that a possible reunion had fallen at the first hurdle.

Two years later, with Jan incapacitated after a near-fatal car accident,
further attempts to revive Focus took place with Thijs and Bert teaming
up with former Earth and Fire guitarist Age Kat. A single session over one
day produced four demos, but once again, the project stalled before it
had begun. Thijs and Jan made another one-off appearance, this time at
the North Sea Jazz Festival in 1993.

During the mid-1990s, Thijs toured with Eef Albers plus a rhythm
section of Bobby Jacobs and Ruben van Roon as the van Leer / Albers

band, playing no classic Focus material. The group recorded another demo, but yet again, the project came to nothing and did not develop into another version of Focus. However, in 1996 another revival was mooted with Thijs, Bert, Hans Cleuver and prodigious young guitarist Menno Gootjes. This line up debuted in August 1997, but it wasn't until the following year that an album and tour was properly mooted. However, Thijs and Bert had a significant difference of opinion, and the tour and album fell through, leaving Hans and the young guitarist understandably furious.

The current version of Focus – which continues at time of writing – first convened in 2001, when Thijs was asked to join Bobby, Ruben van Roon (both members of Thijs side project Conxi) and guitarist Jan Dumee. This band had been playing Focus tunes for fun rather than as a tribute act formed for commercial purposes. This produced immediate interest, both in The Netherlands and abroad, and with van Roon unable to continue with the band, Bert Smaak took over on drums. The new Focus was 'in business'.

Line up changes have seen various members come and go, but the band remain a touring and recording proposition to this day. Pierre van der Linden replaced Smaak in 2004, giving this new version of the band added credibility, and Niels van der Steenhoven replaced Dumee in 2006, later himself to be replaced by a returning Menno Gootjes in 2010. Udo Pannekeet replaced Bobby on bass in 2016. The new band have recorded four albums, *Focus 8* (2002), *Focus 9 / New Skin* (2006), *Focus X* (2012) and *Focus XI* (2019), plus the *Focus Family Album* (2017). The band have also re-recorded the band's greatest hits as *Golden Oldies* (2014) and have also released a couple of other bits and pieces (see Discography).

Jan Akkerman, however, has maintained his career as a respected jazzman, regularly releasing studio and live albums, including the well-received *Close Beauty* in 2019. The question of whether he would consider playing with Thijs again, is one that he is regularly asked, and his reply is a simple one, as reported by Graeme Stroud on the *Velvet Thunder* website in 2019:

Akkerman's relationship with Focus was always a bit tempestuous though, especially with the enigmatic keyboard player, flautist and vocalist of sorts, Thijs van Leer. Akkerman is not wholly resistant to talking about the Focus days; in fact, there are several direct points of reference on the new album (*Close Beauty*), but he approaches talk of his relationship with van Leer tentatively. Nevertheless, the pair have reunited several times over the years for various projects, and I ask if they are happy to play together. 'Oh, no no, there is too much antagonism, you know.' He claims that it doesn't originate so much from his own side, but concludes in full John Cleese mode: 'Don't mention the war, right?'

Buying Focus and the van Leer / Akkerman solo albums

If, like me, you've been following Dutch prog masters Focus for the almost all of the 50 years of their existence, you will have had multiple opportunities to buy the back catalogue. Again, like me, you may have 'replaced' your vinyl copies with CD versions, some released as early as 1987. 2017 saw the Red Bullet label release the *Hocus Pocus Box*, which gathered together the entire back catalogue as it was at that time, from 1969 right into the second decade of the new millennium. This contained thirteen CDs without bonus tracks and a booklet of some (frankly, rather ropey) sleeve notes.

As for the Thijs and Jan solo albums, most have had CD releases over the years via various different labels. For those with deep pockets, an astonishing 26-CD boxed set of Jan's solo albums was released in 2018, compiled and remastered by Wouter Bessels, with many bonus tracks. On a per-CD basis, it's reasonably priced, of course. Only Thijs' solo career has been poorly served by reissues, and some of his albums are almost impossible to find at a reasonable price. However, they are all available on YouTube.

Thijs' *Introspection* series of albums recorded between 1972 and 1979 have been inadequately served by reissues over the years. This is hardly surprising since – of all the music recorded by the two musicians during the 1970s – this project has dated the least sympathetically. I do not hold these albums in contempt. I admire the craft and I have no issues with their commercial intent, but… *caveat emptor*.

Tragically, of Thijs major-label 'pop' excursions, neither *O My Love* or *Nice To Have Met You* have even had CD reissues. While neither would ever get into all-time classic albums lists, there's enough great playing and writing on both to make new editions long overdue.

Returning to Focus, the much-mentioned *Focus 50 Years Anthology 1970-1976* essentially covers the Akkerman era in meticulous, glorious detail. It features all seven of the albums he recorded with the band – including *Live At The Rainbow* and the compilation of outtakes *Ship Of Memories*. However, this time, the albums have been meticulously remastered in their original form, once again by official Focus archivist Wouter Bessels. This includes a return to some original vinyl formatting, so (for instance) 'Anonymus II' from 1972s *Focus 3* has been split in two again as it appeared on the original LP, whereas previous CD versions had it combined into a single, 30-minute piece. He has also returned to the original artwork for the first couple of albums to reflect their original Dutch releases, without forgetting their various other incarnations, of course.

However, the real joy here is in the sumptuous array of bonus material scattered across the seven albums, plus two additional live CDs and – joy of joys – two DVDs, which gather together a great deal of the archive video material from the Akkerman era. Much of this has only been available on BBC compilations or Youtube, and some of it hasn't been seen since it was recorded. The bonus materials may seem a little randomly placed at first until you realise that this is entirely shaped by the 80 minutes available on a single CD. So, *Focus 3* – originally a double album on vinyl – only has room for a few single mixes. Meanwhile, *Focus II / Moving Waves* features an excellent live 'Focus 1' from 1971, while the story continues with *At The Rainbow* and *Ship Of Memories*; the latter, in particular, awash with early and rare versions of familiar favourites, while *Hamburger Concerto* offers up a couple of rare alternative mixes that fans of that album will lap up. *Mother Focus* – the much-derided final album with Akkerman, features various early mixes from that album which, as already mentioned, don't offer many variations of note. But the real treasures are in the four additional discs, which we have already discussed as the tracks crop up in our narrative.

An excellent booklet does a great job in summing up the story and gives some impressive detail about the performances. Finally, the two DVDs also make for fascinating viewing. The first disc covers various performances on the BBC between 1972 and 1974, including the *Live At The Rainbow* set on film, while the second picks up some (but not all) of the archive TV material from Dutch TV, including the 1990 reunion set. The clips include a full 50-minute *Classic Albums* documentary from 1997 concerning *Focus II / Moving Waves*. While it's understandable that this disc should be Dutch-orientated, it's a shame that there are no English subtitles, rendering a great deal of the spoken material unintelligible except for the contributions from English speakers such as Mike Vernon and Jerry Boys. One of the interesting aspects of watching so much material over a short space of time is seeing the deteriorating relationship between Jan Akkeman and Thijs van Leer – their positions on stage move further and further away from each other as the years progress.

But also bear in mind that this set concerns the Akkerman era only, and some might feel that coverage of the Phillip Catherine, Eef Albers and (gulp) P.J. Proby eras would at least complete the Focus story in the 1970s. But these are minor quibbles; this is a remarkable set. If you have albums missing, then this astonishingly good package is the place to go. It's hard to see any reissues – for any band – doing a better job than this, and it's reasonably priced, too.

Selected Compilations

Hocus Pocus – The Very Best Of Focus (1994)
The relatively early compilation, first released on vinyl in the 1970s, and expended for CD in 1994, revived interest in the band during the 1990s, ultimately leading to the revived version of the band that exists at time of writing. It's 'bonus track' – the US single vesion of 'Hocus Pocus' – can also be found on the CD version of *Ship Of Memories*. In truth, there are some odd track selections. 'Mother Focus' is the same track as 'Glider', to all intents and purposes, and some may feel that *Hamburger Concerto* is underrepresented in favour of *Mother Focus*. 'Sneezing Bull' is a major omission. 'Tommy' lovers get a touch more for their money with an extended edit, while others may prefer 'Focus III' without the segue into 'Answers? Questions! Questions? Answers!'. Oh, and the CD mastering error which has the end of 'Anonymus' as the opening moments of 'House Of The King' on the CD of *In And Out Of Focus*' persists here, as the tracks are in the same sequence. Possibly for that very reason.

Thankfully, the 2020 remastered version uses the versions from the *Focus 50 Years Anthology* Box and also corrects the mastering error on the original CD version.

Best of Vol. 2 (2011)
A poorly-packaged and somewhat unnecessary second 'best of' volume released in 2011. It includes most of the rest of the shorter pieces, plus a few more recent tracks. It even has 'Sylvia' and 'Hocus Pocus' live, but *Still* no 'Sneezing Bull.' It's a wasted opportunity.

Golden Oldies (2014)
A very well recorded and played set of classic tracks from the line up as it was in 2014. Some of the versions represent the live versions that the band were playing at the time and are interesting for that reason, while Menno Gootjes on guitar is superb. However, it's unlikely you will stop playing the originals and turn to these versions instead.

Focus Discography 1986 onwards

Focus 8 (2002)
Focus 9 / New Skin (2006)
Focus X (2012)
Focus 8.5 / Beyond the Horizon (2016)
The Focus Family Album (2017)
Focus 11 (2019)

Bibliography And Other Resources

Johnson, Peet., *Hocus Pocus Focus* (Tweed Press, 2015)
Bessels, Wouter., *Focus 50 Years Anthology Box Set Sleeve Notes* (Red Bullet, 2020)
Bessels, Wouter., *Jan Akkerman Remastered CD Sleeve Notes* (Esoteric, 2016)
Daniels, Neil., *Eli / Tabernakel Double CD Sleeve Notes* (BGO, 2015)
Randall, David., *In And Out Of Focus* (SAF Publishing, 2002)
Banks, Peter with James, Billy., *Beyond And Before* (Golden Treasures. 2001)
Stroud, Graeme., Jan Akkerman Inverview at www.velvettunder.co.uk

On Track series

Barclay James Harvest – Keith and Monica Domone 978-1-78952-
The Beatles – Andrew Wild 978-1-78952-009-5
The Beatles Solo 1969-1980 – Andrew Wild 978-1-78952-030-9
Blue Oyster Cult – Jacob Holm-Lupo 978-1-78952-007-1
Kate Bush – Bill Thomas 978-1-78952-097-2
The Clash – Nick Assirati 978-1-78952-077-4
Crosby, Stills and Nash – Andrew Wild 978-1-78952-039-2
Deep Purple and Rainbow 1968-79 – Steve Pilkington 978-1-78952-002-6
Dire Straits – Andrew Wild 978-1-78952-044-6
Dream Theater – Jordan Blum 978-1-78952-050-7
Emerson Lake and Palmer – Mike Goode 978-1-78952-000-2
Fairport Convention – Kevan Furbank 978-1-78952-051-4
Genesis – Stuart MacFarlane 978-1-78952-005-7
Gentle Giant – Gary Steel 978-1-78952-058-3
Hawkwind – Duncan Harris 978-1-78952-052-1
Iron Maiden – Steve Pilkington 978-1-78952-061-3
Jethro Tull – Jordan Blum 978-1-78952-016-3
Elton John in the 1970s – Peter Kearns 978-1-78952-034-7
Gong – Kevan Furbank 978-1-78952-082-8
Iron Maiden – Steve Pilkington 978-1-78952-061-3
Judas Priest – John Tucker 978-1-78952-018-7
Kansas – Kevin Cummings 978-1-78952-057-6
Aimee Mann – Jez Rowden 978-1-78952-036-1
Joni Mitchell – Peter Kearns 978-1-78952-081-1
The Moody Blues – Geoffrey Feakes 978-1-78952-042-2
Mike Oldfield – Ryan Yard 978-1-78952-060-6
Queen – Andrew Wild 978-1-78952-003-3
Renaissance – David Detmer 978-1-78952-062-0
The Rolling Stones 1963-80 – Steve Pilkington 978-1-78952-017-0
Steely Dan – Jez Rowden 978-1-78952-043-9
Thin Lizzy – Graeme Stroud 978-1-78952-064-4
Toto – Jacob Holm-Lupo 978-1-78952-019-4
U2 – Eoghan Lyng 978-1-78952-078-1
UFO – Richard James 978-1-78952-073-6
The Who – Geoffrey Feakes 978-1-78952-076-7
Roy Wood and the Move – James R Turner 978-1-78952-008-8
Van Der Graaf Generator – Dan Coffey 978-1-78952-031-6
Yes – Stephen Lambe 978-1-78952-001-9
Frank Zappa 1966 to 1979 – Eric Benac 978-1-78952-033-0
10CC – Peter Kearns 978-1-78952-054-5

Decades Series

Pink Floyd In The 1970s – Georg Purvis 978-1-78952-072-9
Marillion in the 1980s – Nathaniel Webb 978-1-78952-065-1

On Screen series

Carry On... – Stephen Lambe 978-1-78952-004-0
David Cronenberg – Patrick Chapman 978-1-78952-071-2
Doctor Who: The David Tennant Years – Jamie Hailstone 978-1-78952-066-8
Monty Python – Steve Pilkington 978-1-78952-047-7
Seinfeld Seasons 1 to 5 – Stephen Lambe 978-1-78952-012-5

Other Books

Derek Taylor: For Your Radioactive Children – Andrew Darlington
978-1-78952-
Jon Anderson and the Warriors - the road to Yes – David Watkinson
978-1-78952-059-0
Tommy Bolin: In and Out of Deep Purple – Laura Shenton
978-1-78952-070-5
Maximum Darkness – Deke Leonard 978-1-78952-048-4
Maybe I Should've Stayed In Bed – Deke Leonard 978-1-78952-053-8
The Twang Dynasty – Deke Leonard 978-1-78952-049-1

and many more to come!

Would you like to write for Sonicbond Publishing?

We are mainly a music publisher, but we also occasionally publish in other genres including film and television. At Sonicbond Publishing we are always on the look-out for authors, particularly for our two main series, On Track and Decades.

Mixing fact with in depth analysis, the On Track series examines the entire recorded work of a particular musical artist or group. All genres are considered from easy listening and jazz to 60s soul to 90s pop, via rock and metal.

The Decades series singles out a particular decade in an artist or group's history and focuses on that decade in more detail than may be allowed in the On Track series.

While professional writing experience would, of course, be an advantage, the most important qualification is to have real enthusiasm and knowledge of your subject. First-time authors are welcomed, but the ability to write well in English is essential.

Sonicbond Publishing has distribution throughout Europe and North America, and all our books are also published in E-book form. Authors will be paid a royalty based on sales of their book. Further details about our books are available from www.sonicbondpublishing.com. To contact us, complete the contact form there or email info@sonicbondpublishing.co.uk